No Fear, No Doubt, No Regret

Investing in Life's Challenges like a Warrior

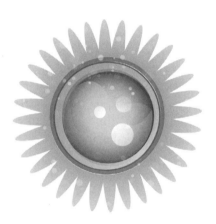

by Robert Omilian

FERNE PRESS

No Fear, No Doubt, No Regret: Investing in Life's Challenges like a Warrior

Summary: A father shares his different insights on life that he learned while raising a disabled child.

Library of Congress Cataloging-in-Publication Data
Omilian, Robert
No Fear, No Doubt, No Regret/Robert Omilian–First Edition
ISBN-13: 978-1-938326-12-7
1. Non-fiction. 2. Parenting a disabled child. 3. Inspiration.
I. Omilian, Robert II. Title
Library of Congress Control Number: 2012951881

FERNE PRESS

Ferne Press is an imprint of Nelson Publishing & Marketing
366 Welch Road, Northville, MI 48167
www.nelsonpublishingandmarketing.com
(248) 735-0418

To all the parents of the world who silently and courageously sacrifice for the good of their children.

Holding an Angel in My Arms

2007

My arms ached, unaccustomed to holding such a weight for any length of time. The veins throbbed, creating a warm tingling sensation up and down my forearms. The nurses worked quickly to clean the bedding below.

"Just a few moments and we will be done," the young nurse with big brown eyes and a freckled nose said in a high-pitched and excited voice. "Are you doing all right?"

Pain suddenly shot through my arms and hands as my focus shifted to my great discomfort.

"No problem."

What else could I say? After all, this was not about me. In comparison to what my son was going through, I had no issues. I held my firstborn son, who was twenty years old. He looked at me and smiled, oh so briefly, as he struggled to breathe.

To ease my pain, I drifted into reverie. Nearly twenty years earlier, I had held Alan in a similar way. I was beaming with pride back then as I took a first look at my new baby boy. He appeared to smile at me then, although it was probably only gas. I remembered the dreams and anticipation I had at his birth, proud to have a son whom I could teach the fine art of baseball, reading, and thinking. I floated as I walked that day, marveling in the new reality that I was now a dad.

A piercing noise screamed from the breathing equipment, jolting me from my memories. The sound punched my head like carpenter's nails, every clang inflicting an even deeper pain in my head and heart. I looked at Alan as he moved his head from side to side, searching for a saving breath. The nurses looked calm, so I pushed my darkest thought back into its cave—the fear of losing my son.

Alan weighed no more than ninety pounds. His face looked like a handsome Russian warrior of the eighteenth century, hair flung back to expose a broad forehead and piercing blue eyes. His square jaw and long but slender nose looked as if they were chiseled from granite to represent this tough and determined soul. His big eyes shimmered like a fresh Wyoming stream. The richness of their color, at that moment, showed me he still had life. Behind those penetrating eyes existed intelligence beyond his years.

In contrast, the rest of his body had suffered the ravages of disease. Muscular neurological myopathy, a form of muscular dystrophy, had twisted his spine, rendering his arms and legs nearly useless, turning his torso in a way that caused a portion of his rib to protrude from his side. I could barely look at his side as I held him in my arms, so I focused only upon his face.

Why had this happened to my son Alan? I asked this over and over. Were twenty years of struggles, amazing successes, bold decisions, and what many would call blind faith about to end?

Just seven days earlier, I happened to run into several of Alan's high school classmates at a restaurant just down the street from the hospital. Their main concern that afternoon was whether they should get a second tattoo on their right arm to match their left arm. Their bodies were bursting with energy. They were very polite to me when they realized who I was, but they never asked about Alan. For four years in high school, these guys sat with Alan in classrooms, helped him maneuver his wheelchair around school, and talked for hours about sports and political issues of the time. In contrast, Alan was lying in a hospital room just several streets away, his head filled with Socrates, Plato, Shakespeare, and Obama, while his body struggled for breath.

Finally the nurses finished their work, and I gently laid Alan back on the bed. He smiled. He could not talk. A long tube protruded from his mouth, providing suction to pull fluids from deep within his lungs.

For several years, Alan had relied upon voice-activated software to write school papers, play fantasy sports, send e-mails to friends, and surf the Internet. Alan had lost the use of his hands years before, making speech his sole method of communication.

After the tube went down his throat, Alan went silent. The free flow of ideas and the excitement of his voice yelling, "Dad, Dad, Dad," to tell me a new idea or fact were not to be heard. Communication was reduced to the nodding of his head. Panic filled those beautiful eyes. Much like a summer electrical brownout, when the lights dim for a brief moment, I saw the shimmer in his eyes disappear, only to reappear a moment later.

◇   ◇   ◇

Alan's resiliency captures the essence of this story. Keeping the glimmer alive in his big blue eyes requires a sacrifice that few parents may willingly accept, but that has provided me with rewards beyond money, fame, or acknowledgment. This resil-

iency in Alan comes from a simple premise that it is not what happens to us but how we respond that defines who we are and influences what happens next.

◊ ◊ ◊

Many people over the years have proclaimed Alan to be the inspirational figure of their lives. But what made Alan to be viewed as such?

In his book titled *Inspiration: Your Ultimate Calling*, Dr. Wayne Dyer wrote about the inspired life. In a passage toward the end of the book, Dr. Dyer said,

> "When I feel inspired, I notice how much zest I have for life and everything that I do: I play tennis with exuberance and without fatigue, I write from my heart—I feel good (God), and this inner feeling radiates outward in all of my waking moments. Inspiration means doing what I love, and even more significantly, loving what I'm doing. It's my willingness to bring love and passion to the activities of my life, rather than looking for love to emerge from those events and activities. It's an attitude, and knowing this, I remember to pick a good one as often as possible. I know that being enthusiastic feels good (God), and I also know that I have the choice to select these attitudes at any and all times. When I stay in-Spirit, these insights on life become second nature to me." (pg 248, July, 2007, Hay House Publishing)

Alan chooses an attitude of love and excitement for life. He continues to choose to focus his attention beyond the daily physical pain and limitations. In looking back over the years, I can identify key insights on life that set the foundation for his choices. These insights have helped my entire family not to merely survive but to thrive in spite of our very trying circumstances. Here are the nine insights that have prepared us for recognizing and acting upon the many blessings which enter our lives on a daily basis:

1. It is not what happens to us but how we respond that defines our existence.

2. Nurture hope and possibilities; a "let's face reality" attitude limits possibilities.

3. Make choices from the heart.

4. Look and listen for the angels who enter our lives; they are daily miracles.

5. Live your dreams, not your troubles.

6. Avoid isolation, the silent enemy.

7. Find the life force in every moment.

8. We cannot predict the journey of our lives; live in awe, wonderment, and thankfulness.

9. Embrace your personal journey.

The coming sections talk about each one of these life-changing insights, providing examples from my experiences with Alan. They provide powerful assistance when dealing with the responsibility of raising children, particularly children with special needs. Throughout the book, I also weave the story of the most recent event for Alan—an event that captures the ninth insight on life: Embrace your personal journey.

2007

As I placed Alan back on the bed, a tear fell upon his face. I sat down on a small, uncomfortable stool next to his bed and placed my throbbing hands over my eyes, using the steadiness of my head to calm my arms. The pulsations I felt were actually soothing: a predictable rhythm of life amidst a turbulent and unpredictable moment.

I closed my eyes for a moment, the warmth of my palms providing comfort to my frazzled heart. The image of several nights before replayed in my mind. The paramedics had arrived around 3:00 a.m. At my request, they spoke calmly and appeared relaxed. I did not want Alan to panic as they prepared to take him to the hospital. A minor issue arose when they wanted to remove him from his trusted motorized wheelchair and place him onto a gurney for the ride to the hospital. The chair, which is painted black and covered with assorted stickers representing various stages of his teen years (Pac Man, sports teams, NASCAR), is literally an extension of his body. Pulling Alan from his trusted chair rips away his independence of movement.

After several short discussions, including a very detailed explanation from the ambulance driver regarding the physics of an ambulance and how his chair could tip over without tie-downs, Alan relented. He likes explanations of facts. Alan advocates for his own rights and needs, never allowing anyone to override his own reasoning abilities.

We wheeled him into the garage, where I lined up the trusty black chair side by side with the gurney. I held Alan's hand as we transferred him. I kissed his forehead, risking his anger at being treated like a baby. Instead, he smiled and looked scared.

The medics quickly loaded him into the ambulance and began hooking up the oxygen. No one knew what was wrong, but Alan's mom, Gwen, had speculated that he could have pneumonia again. She rode with him while I closed the house. I would follow shortly thereafter.

I stood next to Alan's now empty chair, watching from the stark white garage as the ambulance paused for a moment in the street. I could see Alan's head through the side window and wondered if I would ever have him back home. I began to cry as memories of Alan's growing up filled my thoughts. I stood there frozen, until I could no longer see the ambulance.

I felt so lonely standing in that garage. But, just as Alan had taught me over the years, I shook off the sadness, rolled the chair into the van, and set off for the hospital, convinced he would need the chair again. His focus upon possibilities became my focus. For a moment, I could feel him inside me, urging me to get moving. We could not stop now; the journey would continue whether I was ready or not.

Insight 1

It is not what happens to us but how we respond that defines our existence.

The 1987 summer evening had felt endless as we talked with neighbors in our historic neighborhood in Dearborn, Michigan. We shared stories of the latest repairs we'd made to our 1919 homes. We all loved restoring those elegant ladies of the past. Although we sometimes tired of the high level of maintenance required, we felt a sense of commitment to those who had previously cared for our homes. We were continuing the era they had started and felt bonded by this larger sense of purpose.

We were proud to have purchased and restored our two-story early American colonial homes. Our boundless energy fueled a feeling of determination. Weekends transformed us into "do-it-yourself" workers. A caravan of minivans would make the trek to Tele-Warren Lumber to buy pipes, dry wall, wallpaper, and kitchen cabinets. On Saturday evenings, the sound of circular saws, hammers, and the screams of children playing filled the air, and the smells of grilled hamburgers and hot dogs provided the do-it-yourself warriors with a chance to take a break and eat a well-earned meal. We felt prepared and willing to take on any challenge, willing to live an atypical life, symbolized by the sense of community in our historic neighborhood, which was plainly unique from the typical ranch and bungalow homes of our friends.

Gwen felt restless as the last of the neighbors left our backyard. She was eight months pregnant with Alan and decided we needed to walk to the corner ice cream store for our nightly ritual of ultra-rich chocolate cones. The neighborhood streets, guarded by century-old oak trees, felt cool and breezy under the lush midsummer canopy of leaves. The birds were flying all around that night, soaring from tree to tree. The cacophony of their songs overcame the city sounds of cars, sirens, and airplanes just footsteps from our enclave.

While walking from the ice cream store, a thud caused me to turn. It sounded like an apple had fallen, yet no apple trees were near. I looked down and saw a very strange thing— a featherless bird lay squinting at my dirty tennis shoe. He had fallen from the nest. I could hear his faint chirping while his fragile legs flailed in the air. His skin was so thin that we could see right through him as he lay prostrate before us. We did not know what to do. As we entered our backyard, we kept talking about this little bird, speculating over his fate.

That little bird haunted my thoughts. I tried to settle down for the evening in my lounge chair on the deck. I crossed my legs, uncrossed them, walked around the darkened yard, closed the garage for the evening, and poured myself some lemonade. The little bird kept coming to mind. Finally, I told Gwen I was going to go back for him. With an old shoebox in hand, I retraced our path down the now dark street. I walked slowly, fearing I might step on my featherless friend.

As I approached what I thought to be the spot, a tiny miracle occurred: a car turning the corner shone its lights on the ground just as I looked down. I swept the little bird into my shoebox and rushed home. I had no idea what I would do to keep him alive, but at least I had pulled him out of the darkness and into the light of my garage.

I tried feeding him milk and small bird food, but nothing worked. I had no clue what to do, so I called the local veterinarian. He advised letting the little bird pass away naturally, believing nothing could be done. For days the little guy lived in the old shoebox, chirping away every time I entered the garage. Even though my efforts seemed futile, I carried on and he became part of my routine for several weeks. One day the little one died, but not before I had named him Miracle and lovingly stroked his tiny head nightly to calm him and coax him to eat. After his death, even though I missed his chirping when I exited the car, a peaceful feeling came over me when I reflected upon my naïve attempt to save this little creature against such odds. Little did I know this bird served as an omen of things to come. The love we showed Miracle made a difference in our lives, revealing a passion within us to never give up, walk away, or ignore a situation that appears difficult to handle.

Several weeks later Gwen gave birth to Alan, three weeks early. He looked beautiful and energetic, yet frail. As Alan made his entrance into the world from his mother's womb, his right hand tightly holding the umbilical cord, I instantly realized how little my existence mattered. My son became my reason for living.

Alan showed the awareness of older babies. As he grew stronger, he observed everything with unlimited energy. He was forever curious about his new world. Gwen and I took

Alan everywhere. Weekends were flat-out travel events to the zoo, museums, parks, and friends' homes. We lived to celebrate our new boy.

Often we walked our neighborhood after work, Alan wide awake in his stroller. He looked here and there, fighting our feeble attempts to tire him out. When he began to use words, his first expression was "go, go" whenever we slowed down for a traffic light or a conversation with a neighbor. Alan wanted action all the time. In honor of this, we began calling Alan our "Go-Go Baby."

Throughout his first year, Alan developed into a plump little boy who never tried to crawl, pull himself up, or walk. He preferred scooting to get his toys. Our families criticized Gwen and me for holding him too much, preventing him from naturally wanting to stand and walk. Unfortunately, Alan's developmental issues dwarfed those simple-minded comments.

On Alan's first birthday, after all the family and friends had said goodbye, Alan suddenly developed a terrible fever of 104°F. He had received one of his childhood immunization shots just three days earlier, so we thought he was having a reaction. The doctor suggested we cool Alan down with a bath and bring him to the office in the morning or take him to the emergency room if the fever did not subside. Alan did cool down rapidly with the sponge bath and everything seemed fine that night.

The next day at the doctor's office, our pediatrician zeroed in on the fact that Alan wasn't walking and hadn't even tried to walk. We wanted to know about the fever, but the doctor had larger concerns in mind. She noted a slight separation at the tailbone, which she thought might be preventing his walking. She took X-rays and wanted us to visit frequently until Alan began to walk. Little did we realize that this doctor visit would be the beginning of a long quest for answers on an ever-increasing list of questions regarding his physical development.

Within two months, Alan began to walk. But then his feet started pointing outward. A foot specialist concluded Alan's tendons had not yet tightened to pull his feet back. Another group of doctors began observing Alan, focusing upon his feet.

Alan improved, but his feet corrected slowly. He walked with an uneasy gait, almost as if one leg were longer than the other.

In the midst of our growing concern about his physical development, Alan's endless energy and love for life emerged stronger than ever. His curiosity and determination drove him to do things beyond his physical capabilities. I still break out in a sweat when I recall Alan riding on the merry-go-round. He would hold on, but I never knew if he could sustain his grip to avoid flying off the ride. Alan also climbed the tallest heights of playscapes, determined to keep pace with the older kids.

◇   ◇   ◇

Achievement and adventure motivate Alan to this day, creating constant tension between his growing physical limitations and his expanding intellectual capability and boundless energy. Over the years, this tension has driven many of the turning points and achievements in his life.

The first time this tension mattered was when Alan was in preschool. We found a place with a wonderful teacher eager to accept Alan. Several months into the school year, the school had a father-child night. Alan was so proud to take me into his classroom. The teacher had twenty-five activities for the fathers to do with their children within a one-hour period—a lot to accomplish within a short period of time. The activities included drawing leaves, pasting sticks together to build forts, planting flowers, and drawing our body outline on a large sheet of paper. The teacher made it clear that we did not have to do all the activities, just what we felt comfortable doing.

I asked Alan which activities he wanted to do. He looked at me for quite awhile without saying a word, struggling to find an answer. The rest of the dads were already off doing the activities when Alan finally said, "Let's do all of the events." I wanted to object, but decided to keep quiet. His determination moved us along and actually made it fun. I relaxed and began looking for a few corners to cut so we could achieve his goal. With no time left, I used my best pitiful-sounding voice on the teacher to squeeze out a few extra minutes. We planted a flowering plant that would eventually go to Gwen weeks later for mom's night.

◊　◊　◊

Alan's determination that night spoke volumes about who he is. He does not dwell upon his physical limitations but rather keeps his eye on the goal. He never wants to miss out on anything, wishing to experience every opportunity to the fullest. This ability to focus upon the goal—to imagine the possibilities—helps Alan to minimize obstacles by looking past them. This has taught me a lesson. With Alan's physical disease unrelenting in its march toward his destruction, I need to be sure that Alan's goals are clear. When they are clear, we always have something to strive for, which allows us to transcend his physical limitations.

With life and its outcome so unpredictable, what matters most is not so much what happens but how we respond when life makes a move on us. During the first twenty years of our journey, Alan's natural tendency to focus upon his response to circumstances instead of what has happened to him physically emerges as one of the true constants. He has bounced back so often from physical setbacks, emerging stronger in spirit and determination to achieve his goals. This resiliency makes Alan an inspirational figure to those who know him, often giving strength to those physically stronger.

A Parent's Thoughts

Do I spend too much time focusing upon what is lacking in my children? Is my response to difficulties negative and self-defeating? How do I make my response more focused upon possibilities, given the circumstances and conditions?

Have you noticed that people who always view the glass as half-empty are seen as the realists, the practical ones who are well-grounded? Somehow, optimism and choosing to look for the positive in life are seen as unrealistic. Yet how much opportunity is lost by focusing upon the restrictions of a situation instead of the possibilities?

Insight 2

Nurture hope and possibilities; a "let's face reality" attitude limits possibilities.

One spring morning in April 1990, Alan and I sat in the dining room of our home. We felt sunshine pour through the tall windows. A warm breeze blew the old-fashioned lace curtains against my back. The neighborhood children screamed in high-pitched voices, riding their bicycles and throwing baseballs in the street.

I sat that morning thinking about the visit to the doctor's we'd made the day before. A foot specialist had examined Alan's feet, trying to understand why his right foot curved out and was not correcting over time. He suggested an operation to pull the ligaments together but could not explain why the ligaments were so loose. This doctor became the first to suggest that Alan might have a serious illness. My fighter's response had taken over. "Not my son," I thought. "I WILL NOT LET THIS HAPPEN TO HIM." Yet I had no idea what to do. I still had no idea what was wrong.

In the middle of my reverie, Alan looked at me and said, "So, what do you think, Dad?"

I chuckled. Alan had a wonderful glow in his big three-year-old blue eyes. He sat forward in his blue booster chair and stared at me, anticipating an answer. His long, skinny legs dangled from the chair, swinging back and forth in anticipation of something. Alan's body filled with energy when he became excited or curious.

I asked him, "About what?"

He just kept looking at me for a moment, feet still dangling, and asked again, "So, what do you think?"

When I asked again about what, he responded, "Everything!"

Everything! Think about sharing what we think about everything. Where would I begin and how would I respond appropriately to a three-year-old child? That event was the first of what became many moments when Alan opened my mind to possibilities just by using a certain phrase. In this instance, Alan's asking me to speak about "everything" made me consider how my opinions developed over time from my experiences and from the influence of parents, family, and friends. Some of these opinions, when exposed to the light of explanation, appear naïve. Other opinions appear wise. But above all of that, I discovered my right to my opinions and choices, even when faced with seemingly intolerable circumstances. Thinking about "everything" placed the present doctor's opinion in a larger context. My spirits lifted. For one hour, I discussed what I thought about the house, his mother, his baby brother, Andy, the doctors, baseball, summer trips around the country, work, and whatever else came to mind.

Alan listened to it all, his blue eyes radiating with life. He never asked to get down from his chair. I paused frequently to give him a chance to say "enough" and run off and play. It never happened. He wanted to hear what he thought were his dad's secrets.

◊　◊　◊

The "So, what do you think?" question reveals a truth. Even when faced with troubling news, I have a choice to look around for alternatives or accept what's been given to me. I even have the ability to give myself a break from worrying, to clear my thoughts, and to mentally breathe. I have discovered that forming opinions and looking at my thoughts are vital when managing difficult circumstances. It calms me down, allowing new feelings and ideas to enter my mind. In all, I can avoid feeling like a victim to the doctors' continuous questioning and testing of Alan.

◊　◊　◊

I began to feel the power of choice while facing the fear of the unknown. I could still choose to be hopeful. I could also choose to take control of the doctors, giving them a task to work on together in order to understand Alan's problems.

One day Alan, Gwen, and I were invited to a doctors' symposium at the Detroit Children's Hospital. The guest speakers included a doctor from the Mayo Clinic in Minnesota. We sat through several lectures regarding muscular dystrophy. Finally, the guest speaker from Minnesota came up to talk. He specialized in the theory of how the immune system attacks the body. The doctor was a tall and husky man, with large hands like a basketball player. He spoke rather slowly and deliberately, with an air of self-assurance that struck me as somewhat arrogant. But he was speaking before a hundred or so doctors, each of whom had a theory. His air of superiority required the audience to be attentive, if for no other reason than to identify points of disagreement. Toward the end of his presentation, Alan was invited to the front, along with me, to present Alan's case to this man.

I felt like I was before the tribal king, begging for permission to receive his grand wisdom. The auditorium's theater lights were turned directly upon us. The sound of the doctors moving forward in the auditorium to get a closer view of the show broke what had been a library-like hush while the doctor spoke. I whispered to Gwen that we were the lab rats for the day. Our doctor presented a very concise summary of Alan's tests and the results. I was asked to take Alan's shoes and socks off and have him walk across the floor so all could see his gait. We rolled up Alan's sleeves so his skin color and texture could be observed and felt. After a few more minutes of questions and sidebar conversations among the doctors, the master guest was ready to provide his verdict, or, I mean, his analysis of Alan's condition. He proclaimed that Alan did not suffer from an immune system attacking itself but rather had a disease that attacked the nervous system and would lead to an overall weakness in his body but should not threaten his life. He spoke of a young woman who had similar symptoms and lived her adult life independently, requiring only the aid of a dog as her companion and support.

I must admit that I felt comfortable with this doctor's analysis. He reviewed the test charts and then restated his view. At the end of the review, our doctor came to us and expressed his doubts about this evaluation. I moved from the hope that finally we were hearing a concrete diagnosis to despair that we were just objects of disagreement. These folks did not know what was going wrong for Alan. My son's life was apparently threatened by some mysterious disease and I could do nothing but be an object of discussion and debate while the cruel force of nature destroyed my precious son's body.

"So, what do you think?" came to mind, reminding me that even though those wonderful doctors were the experts and deserved respect, I also had an opinion. I did not need to feel like a helpless victim; instead, I could use the experience to further my understanding of Alan's illness.

The idea that Alan's immune system was attacking him in reaction to a virus in his body had the most support from testing, but the treatments led to the greatest physical deterioration. Treatments, in general, have not worked to reverse or stop the physical deterioration of his body. The medical procedures and endless theories over what could be going wrong have caused the most stress for us all.

◇　◇　◇

In addition to exercising my right to have an opinion, I have found another way to reclaim a feeling of control: take action, do something to feel alive. Too much thinking about a problem can quickly lead to feelings of depression.

◇　◇　◇

One way we began to reclaim our lives from this grip of fear was by deciding to go on road trips around the country. These trips, if nothing else, gave us a break from focusing on the seriousness of Alan's condition. I also believe these adventures to parts unknown instilled a healing energy in Alan, giving him the power to overcome his physical constraints.

We drove everywhere over a period of ten years, bringing back the 1960s-style family road trip. The first year's journey was to Disney World in Orlando, Florida. Alan was seven and our second son, Andy, was five. We spent days preparing for the trip and had the car loaded and ready to go the night before. When the day came to leave, we jumped into the blue Taurus station wagon and drove off.

Before we left on this first of many trips around the United States, I looked in the rearview mirror to check on the boys. When I shifted my eyes toward Alan, I saw the most beautiful image, one from which I have gained personal strength in the years since: Alan's blue eyes, sandwiching a freckled nose, focused upon the road ahead. His face glowed from feelings of anticipation, wonder, and hope for new things to see and understand. My rearview-mirror glimpse of Alan's face comforted me on that trip. I checked often to see if the look remained. It did. Alan read all the signs to me and kept asking questions about what would come next. His energy gave me hope that, somehow, his physical illness would be overcome.

One hot July day, Alan's doctor arranged a series of electrical-stimulation tests. I arrived late to the session, having been delayed at work with meetings. Alan was in tears and was screaming because the electrical shocks hurt so badly. I asked the doctor to hook me up so I could feel the effect. Was I crazy? This might hurt! But then I stopped my thoughts and told myself it was exactly what I wanted to do so that I could experience what Alan was feeling. And I thought it might also give Alan a bit more courage. The pain played tricks, delaying the effect of its strength until I began to think it did not exist. But then the pain suddenly emerged like a glowing, red-hot rod, slowly getting hotter until the growing warmth and sting permeated my entire body. My ears began to ring and I could not say exactly where the pain came from. It just filled my entire being. But I kept a strong face. Alan did take comfort in seeing that I had survived.

We had to get those tests completed somehow.

On the way to the doctor's office, I had heard a report about the Cincinnati Reds baseball team. The reporter spoke about the team's chances of winning that year. While the doctors re-hooked Alan up for the tests, I started telling Alan about the report. He immediately began talking about what he had heard, spouting facts I never knew existed about the Reds. He completely forgot about the tests, and we managed to get through the rest of the shocks while Alan continued to talk about baseball. His power of concentration overcame that glowing heat shooting through his body, demonstrating a power far beyond what I would have expected him to be capable of at the age of eight.

Bob, Alan, and Andy, 1985. Picture taken at Uncle Ron's wedding engagement party. Alan is eight years old and Andy is six years old.

The baseball discussion not only took Alan's mind off of the physical pain, it connected him to what he loves. It brought him back to his dreams and passions. The baseball talk allowed him to project beyond—way beyond—his physical condition. While he talked, the look of anticipation came back to his eyes. He asked if we could visit Cincinnati's ballpark.

"Of course," I said. "How about this weekend?"

The "look of Alan" came back stronger than ever.

I have used this "look of Alan" for years to help me decide what is best to do. Keeping this look alive has led us to do things which, it has turned out, have frequently been choices of the heart, actions that many probably have thought were a waste of time and money, given the situation. But as long as my goal was to keep that look alive in Alan, then money and time diminished in importance, with the reward being that beautiful look in Alan's mighty blue eyes.

A Parent's Thoughts

I can give Alan a sense of hope only if I truly feel hopeful. I can choose to be hopeful anytime I wish. It becomes a choice, one that can open up experiences and meaning beyond anything I might anticipate.

The Struggle for Hope

2007

When I arrived at the University of Michigan emergency room, Alan looked calm. Gwen held Alan's hand and silently listened to the discussions of the medical staff as they tried to identify why Alan was so short of breath.

"He may come home today," Gwen said in a monotone voice, conveying to me rather succinctly what the doctor had been saying and her assessment of how possible it might be. Although it was what I wanted to hear, she and I both understood how quickly things could change. But hope is a great thing, and it has carried us through many difficult moments, giving us the sense that we might have some control over life.

Finally, the head doctor arrived. He talked with Alan for a few moments, looked at the charts, came back to observe other things, and then disappeared behind the cloth screen. Within moments, he returned to say that Alan would be admitted to the hospital for observation. His blood oxygen level was low but improving. The doctor wanted to see it stabilized.

That night, I sat with Alan. We talked about baseball and basketball for half the night. I was trying to wear him down so he could sleep. However, the longer he stayed awake, the more difficult it became for him to relax. The doctor decided to give him a mild sleeping pill. He did sleep for one hour. Then events turned ugly.

I tried to sleep. The machine that kept track of Alan's heart rate, blood pressure, and blood oxygen levels lured me into its instant-update world, much like a stock market ticker. I craved more updates just to verify that Alan was safe. I looked for patterns in the data that would indicate improvement.

When I saw that the key indicators were stable, I would close my eyes to sleep, believing the instant-update machine would alert me if anything changed. Then one of the key data points tripped the alarm. First the oxygen count dipped below 88, sending out a piercing alarm. Then the blood pressure alarm sounded. I ignored this one, since the blood pressure device had malfunctioned several times earlier.

But then the heart rate indicator sounded. I awoke from my shallow sleep to see the rate increasing rapidly, although Alan still slept and appeared to be calm. 90, 95, 100, 120, 130 went the readings, all within one minute. His heart rate stayed steady at 130 for a few moments. A doctor came in, observed, and left, then sent an intern into the room to monitor the situation. Then his heart rate shot up to 140, 150, 160. Suddenly the room filled with doctors and nurses. Alan awoke, startled by the commotion. When the reading hit 180, Alan looked at me. He just stared into my eyes, using me as a gauge for what was happening. I tried to smile and keep him calm. The lead doctor came to me and said he was going to give Alan a beta blocker to slow down his heart rate and prevent a heart attack.

I felt panic in my gut. My young son was having a heart attack!!! No way could this be happening! I felt so helpless at his side. I held Alan's hand just in case things went suddenly wrong; Alan needed to know he was not alone.

His heart rate did return to normal. Dehydration had been the cause for the rate increase. Alan returned to sleep. I, on the other hand, felt dizzy. I was sweating with fear over what might have happened. I felt nauseated. Had I just come close to losing my son? Tears started to flow uncontrollably. But I did not care. I sat next to Alan and held his hand close to my heart.

Gwen arrived at the hospital at 6:00 a.m. I explained what had happened, gave her a big kiss, and left for home. I had grown up believing I needed to control life and its events in order to be successful. I clearly had zero control to slow down Alan's heart rate. I had stood by, feeling like a useless person, watching events unfold as if I were watching a television show. My head continued to spin as I drove home. No matter what I thought, no matter how clever I tried to be, I could not shake the feeling of powerlessness.

The next day while I slept, Alan's condition worsened. The mucus in his lungs exploded in quantity, essentially suffocating Alan from within. With caution still in the air over the previous night's heart-rate incident, the doctor wanted to provide Alan immediate relief for his breathing in order to keep pressure off of his heart.

At noon, Gwen called. The doctor had just placed a tube down Alan's throat to provide oxygen deep inside his lungs and to create a path for pulling the mucus out. Alan could not talk with this tube down his throat.

When I arrived that evening, Gwen warned me of Alan's mood; he was depressed and frustrated. Gwen had struggled all day to understand what he needed. Alan could not write due to the weakness in his arms. All he had were head movements and his eyes to communicate.

I had no idea what he was trying to tell me.

NO WAY CAN I BE CLUELESS, I thought.

Yet I might as well have been looking at a complete stranger. We assume we know our spouse and children so well that we can understand their needs no matter what the circumstance may be.

A young nurse came into the room just as I was about to scream in frustration over my inability to understand Alan. She wanted to hook up the television and needed to know if Alan wanted several pieces of electronic equipment to aid him. She could not understand him either. She looked to me for help. "I have no clue," I said to her.

Alan uses words very well. He develops complex ideas and needs, and the complexity of his needs requires articulate communication. For example, a request for a drink is typically a request for an ice-cold Dr. Pepper in a cup with a bendable straw. Do not bend the straw too far for fear of any liquid spilling on one of his many sports jerseys. Turning on the television is not adequate. He specifically requests the channels that have his favorite sports teams or he wants to watch a particular cable news station to follow his political passion.

The tube in his throat complicated his needs. The young nurse tried to interpret what Alan was asking for. We could not read his lips either. I had never thought reading lips would be difficult until I had to try. Alan was using very long and complex words and sentences rather than simple words. He, too, was struggling to get us dummies to understand what he wanted.

The nurse had an idea. She pulled out a chart of letters. With this and a blank sheet of paper, she went one letter at a time to spell words. Alan nodded his head when she pointed to the correct letter.

Never had Alan and I felt as frustrated with each other as we did at that moment. We actually swore at each other—this was quite easy to interpret from Alan's lips. We worked at the chart, quit for a moment, and then tried again.

Alan looked exhausted after a half-hour of trying this. The doctors were asking him to try harder at pulling out the mucus. They wanted him to push himself. I tried to explain that his will to achieve exceeded that of anyone else. But it appeared he had lost hope.

I began talking to him about trying harder when he finally shook his head abruptly from right to left, over and over again. I did not understand what he wanted.

He kept doing it, so I finally asked, with irritation, "What is it that you want?"

He nodded toward the sheet of letters. One by one I pointed to each letter until he nodded "JUSTLEAVE-MEALONE."

For the first time in twenty years, it looked like Alan had lost hope.

Insight 3

Make choices from the heart.

All of the physical deterioration, testing, probing, and prodding of Alan left me feeling powerless. Hour upon hour I sat watching, listening to the theories, and waiting for results. I had spent hundreds of dollars on Band-Aids, knee protectors, and braces to keep Alan safe while his body grew taller and more likely to fall over the smallest thing on the floor. Nightly I spent hours exercising Alan, using large balls for him to roll on, putting books in his hands to carry for strengthening his arms, and having him kick soccer balls to maintain leg strength. In spite of all this, the disease kept charging onward.

One thing I had control over was keeping Alan positive and focused on what he could do. I may not have known what the physical disease was, but I did know Alan's brilliance. He craves knowledge and the debate of ideas with others. Alan's face glows with excitement by learning a new fact, hearing a news story on National Public Radio, or debating the latest political controversy. His energy improves when he is excited by intellectual challenges. Alan's mind appears to be near photographic. He writes outstanding essays and loves to engage in conversation. Since fifth grade, all his IQ tests and achievement-related tests have indicated that he has genius-level capability.

Alan's educational opportunities became an area I could influence. Schools, therefore, were significant. The choice of his high school, in particular, was a most significant turning point in our life.

On a windy, wet, and cold Thursday in November of 2000, Gwen and I drove our sons to their grade school and then headed for one more interview session with a local high school to determine whether they would work with us to achieve our goals.

Alan had started to use a wheelchair full-time when he was in the seventh grade. His ability to write and feed himself had diminished rapidly. Prior to seventh grade, the major issues had been Alan's physical safety, namely, not falling down stairs or into sharp objects like desks and doors. With the wheelchair, his physical safety improved, but his ability to compete in the classroom became the problem.

Alan's inability to feed himself or take notes in class started to create barriers to his education. The principal at his grade school could not adjust to his growing physical needs. Alan had always been one of the top students in the school, enjoyed many friends, and had planned to use seventh and eighth grade to further establish himself as one of the best students among a class of very bright and gifted children. The principal wanted to move Alan to a school where public funds could provide for a full-time aide to take notes for him and help him eat lunch. Several teachers became convinced that if Alan continued to do well in school, parents would think he had been given assistance. Their reasoning was that if a physically impaired child performed better in the classroom than a child who could take his or her own notes, then it would appear that some exceptions had been made.

Alan did continue to do very well in all subjects with only the help of friends taking notes for him. His success did create silent suspicion among several parents. Alan's arriving one to two minutes late to the classroom due to the extra time it took to move his wheelchair through the hallways drew severe responses from one teacher and from the principal. His occasional need to be out of school for a doctor's appointment became further reason to question the appropriateness of his being in that particular school. The principal refused to provide a special parking spot near the school entrance because it would interfere with the flow of other cars.

Although Alan had to dictate his essays and test answers to his teacher, no extra time was allowed, even though it took more time to dictate a math answer than it would have taken him to actually write the answer.

In spite of all this, Alan continued to excel. Several very special friends continued to be with him and treated him as if nothing were wrong or difficult. The majority of the parents loved having Alan in the school and made very special efforts to help when they could. Soon, though, the reality became a paradox. In order to be considered equal in achievement to the non–physically challenged kids, Alan had to live up to a higher standard than the other kids. Although it took Alan longer to write due to his weakening hands, he had to write the test in the same amount of time as the other kids; essentially, he had less time to consider answers. This meant he had a much tougher standard, which was equivalent to cutting the non–physically challenged kids' time in half and expecting them to produce the same results.

His eighth-grade graduation trip encapsulated the conflicting attitudes we lived with during those final two years of grade school. The trip consisted of a two-day whirlwind event, via buses, from Detroit to Chicago, where the kids and select parents visited the Shedd Aquarium, ate at popular restaurants, attended a theater production for kids, and spent time in the hotel swimming pool. On the day of the trip, the principal told me that the buses did not have handicap accessibility. When I asked her why, she told me that she had not been sure I wanted Alan to go, even though I had sent in the confirmation form and requested a handicap-accessible bus. I still did not understand her motives, but there was no way I was going to prevent Alan from going with his friends and celebrating his eight years of grade school. I told her I would drive Alan in my van and follow the bus to Chicago and back.

Driving behind two buses in rush-hour traffic in Chicago can be very difficult. Many opportunities existed to get lost due to traffic lights or traffic movement. Alan felt humiliated at being singled out. All the parents knew it and were very supportive of us as we followed behind in our van.

On the first day in Chicago, we did lose the buses. I knew, in general, where the restaurant was located; I just kept driving, hoping to spot them. We finally turned onto a large, busy street and there stood several dads in the middle of the street, waiting for me. They had held up traffic so that I could make the quick maneuver I needed to get the parking spot they had held for me. These dads had jumped off the bus when they realized I was no longer behind them and had made sure I could easily find them. They continued to do this throughout the rest of the trip, always making sure that Alan was included in all events.

The love and respect shown by these parents and Alan's friends kept us in that school during those final two years, but we had to make the transition to high school. Would we be able to keep Alan in the best school available, public or private, without subjecting him to the lack of attention he received from the grade school principal and select teachers?

One school we visited in 2001 had a reputation for being the best for boys who want to excel intellectually and athletically. The school, Catholic Central High School (CC), functions as an all boys' school. I had attended the school and had always hoped my sons would, too. We had previously visited the public high school. They had an excellent program designed to provide Alan all-day assistance with note-taking and bathroom needs. They also had an honors program designed for kids like Alan who were bright and motivated. There was no tuition, which appealed to us. But something appeared to be missing. It might have been my bias after having been educated in private schools. CC would be the last school we visited before making a decision.

Alan insists upon no special favors, just a fair chance to achieve, based upon his ability. He wants to be in what many call "mainstream," and doesn't want to be pulled aside in a separate-but-equal arrangement. He wants to challenge himself against the brightest, handicap or not.

Catholic Central offered a very competitive, intellectual environment where friendships, brotherhood, and a love for knowledge were the motivating factors for most of the students and faculty. Alan would be in classes with all the students, not in a separate program. The physical arrangements needed would be the most significant barrier. As a private school, CC did not have the resources to provide a full-time aide and specially funded computer programs.

Gwen and I stopped in front of the building and looked at the school. Could this be it? The famous CC? The place where young men consistently rank in the top one percent in the state of Michigan for national achievement awards? This building looked small in comparison to the public high school. Although it was clean and well-kept, the place looked old.

As we entered the main door, we immediately recognized what the school did not have in comparison to the public high school. There was no main auditorium, cafeteria, or radio station. The CC cafeteria served as a meeting room, auditorium, and makeshift classroom when needed. This cafetorium, as they called it, at the very front of the building was enclosed by glass and aluminum wall grids. We also noticed the silence and lack of students wandering around during class time.

After taking only a few steps into the building, we were greeted by a friendly voice. "You must be the Omilians. I have been looking forward to meeting you."

Hearing the phrase "Looking forward to meeting you" felt refreshing. They already knew the circumstances we could be bringing to them, based on a telephone call I had made a month earlier. The assistant principal, Dave, welcomed us into his office. I had prepared my usual speech describing Alan's condition and what we wished to accomplish for him—a chance to achieve intellectually on merit in an environment where he would be part of the whole community all of the time, and an appreciation for his physical constraints with accommodations made where needed. Before I could begin, Dave started to explain the pre-work he and the staff had done. He paused before diving into the details and said the school had never enrolled a student with a disability similar to Alan's and was not sure they had the right resources to appropriately handle the situation effectively. But given Alan's academic achievements in grade school and the results of the entrance exam, the school absolutely wanted him to attend and was willing to do whatever it took to help him be successful. He thanked us for giving CC a chance to make it work.

We did not know how to respond. After two years of rejection and contempt from the grade school principal, we were shocked and relieved by what Dave told us. He then continued to describe what they could do. Actions included providing a special parking spot outside the door, widening the bathroom door for his chair, moving all of Alan's classes to the first floor, allowing him to dictate tests to the librarian, educating the staff on Alan's needs, and storing special nutrition drinks in the cafeteria. Students would be expected to take notes for Alan and help him with lunch. The only thing they could not handle was bathroom needs.

To address the bathroom needs, I would have to come to the school during my lunchtime and help. The school would provide two sets of textbooks—one for home and one for school. A special area in each classroom would be available for Alan to wheel in and stretch out, typically near the door, but he would always be surrounded by other students so that he wouldn't feel isolated.

Following the meeting, we walked slowly toward our car. We paused, looked back at the building, and had a different view of the school. Rather than seeing it as looking old and small, we began to understand how it could feel like home, a place where love and caring transformed the old school into a building filled with energy and hope. Gwen began to cry. She immediately felt CC had shown love for our son, even before they had met him.

We did not talk to Alan too much about what we had experienced. We wanted him to visit the public school and CC so he could determine where he felt comfortable. After visiting the two schools, Alan had several unexpected insights. He felt very comfortable at the public high school. They had all the concerns covered. Alan would have an aide with him full-time. The staff had shown excitement about the prospect of having him there and indicated he would be able to socialize with the other kids. Because of Alan's intelligence, he would be in the honors program. When he visited CC for the open house, Alan had several major concerns regarding who would take care of him during the day and who would take notes for him in the classroom. Yet he did like the feeling of tradition and brotherhood at the school.

The Catholic Central open house proved to be the defining moment. Hundreds of eighth graders filled the school halls, their parents walking behind them, all of them wondering what was so special about the place. Upperclassmen gave presentations about subjects ranging from math to Latin, chess club to football team tryouts. Every presenter talked about key awards the school had received over the years. The accomplishments of the school and the way the students conducted themselves started to convince the parents and eighth graders about the significance of CC.

During the tour, one of the upperclassmen took it upon himself to assume care for Alan. He pushed the wheelchair around corners, sat with him during the presentations, collected all the literature, and fed him cookies and pop at the social. His name was Ben and he loved sports. Ben and Alan talked baseball and football for a long time. Alan was animated. He talked for hours after the open house about the classes he heard the students talk about, the special school songs, sports championships, and academic honors. He started talking about the classes he would take.

In spite of the aides available at the public high school, Alan chose CC. He felt, as we had after our first visit, that the school offered more than just opportunities to have assistance for his physical needs. CC made Alan feel like he would have opportunities to compete academically with the best in mainstream society. He realized that he would be separate but equal at the public high school—he would be in the mainstream classes but would be inherently separated by the constant presence of adult aides. Lunch would be with other physically disabled kids so the aides could accommodate them all at once. But the overall feeling he had about CC was that they would take care of him. Ben had made him believe in the school. This faith was what began to drive Alan.

The decision regarding high school became, in essence, a spiritual choice. Alan would not have chosen to attend Catholic Central if we had taken all the practical pluses and minuses and added them up. The choice came down to a more intuitive process; our sense of the possibilities available for Alan guided the decision. His face beamed with anticipation and vitality, much like the look of anticipation and excitement I had seen in the rearview mirror before we left on our vacations. Seeing that look of life confirmed, for me, that CC would keep that look alive and well. I needed nothing more to convince me than to see that expression on his face when he talked about the joy he felt regarding his opportunities at CC. The energy that filled him as he anticipated his high school years overshadowed any of the physical destruction to his body, which continued relentlessly.

On the first day of school at CC, I wanted to watch from a distance to see how he handled lunch. I poked my head into the cafeteria from a back door entrance so Alan wouldn't see me. I scanned the room, filled with guys who were boasting about events and laughing loudly. I could not see Alan. I looked for, but couldn't find, his black wheelchair. In my head, I was running through several scenarios about where he could be when a group of students huddled around the table immediately in front of me caught my attention. I could see one rather large kid wearing a football jersey, reaching over the table. I stepped into the room and finally saw Alan, right in the middle of those five kids, talking away while they fed him his lunch and ate their own lunch. What struck me most was how they made no big deal over feeding him. The one guy just reached over to Alan as effortlessly as he could while feeding himself, still talking all the time.

I walked over to the nearest teacher and asked him if he had arranged for Alan to be fed by the kids at that table. He looked at me like I had no clue.

Alan, Gwen, and Andy, 2001. Alan's freshman year in high school.

"Oh no, a bunch of students asked to help Alan with lunch. I had to help him handle the situation. He did not want to insult any of them by having to choose. So we decided that each one would take a day of the week to eat lunch with Alan."

I was truly speechless, finally understanding. I quickly sank back into the shadows of the doorway so as not to be seen. I pulled out my cell phone and called Gwen.

"You will not believe what I just saw. No, Alan is fine. In fact, he had to make a tough decision today. No, no, nothing bad. He had to choose who would feed him lunch. Several guys volunteered. No, the teachers did not force them. He is coming now; I have to go. Can you believe that?"

The students' immediate acceptance of Alan did more for him than anything else I could ever have imagined. I do not know what his life would be like if we had not chosen Catholic Central. Sure, I had to spend four years traveling through ice, snow, rain, and summer heat to his school at lunchtime. The homework we had to do with Alan made me feel like I was back in school. At times, I wished I had state-funded assistance to rely upon for those homework needs. Yet when I look back at those four years, the tough nights of homework seem very short-lived when compared to Alan's academic growth.

I never realized what a difference a choice can make until I experienced Alan's high school years with him. I have learned that we can make choices between opportunities and possibilities. Opportunities for advancement, money, love, and so on exist within the context of a person's present view of reality. We make these choices based on what seems to be most logical and prudent, given the conditions. However, there will always be a choice that creates possibilities for something else, something beyond the present moment of reality. Some refer to this kind of choice as an action of vision. People who consistently choose this type of action are often called visionaries and leaders. To choose opportunities instead of possibilities is less risky and would probably meet the approval of prudent people. Choosing possibilities may have more risks, but the risks ignite energy and growth to achieve things that at first might not seem possible. To identify possibilities when they appear and have the courage to act upon them is the trickier part of life.

In Alan's case, we could have chosen the opportunity at the public high school, where he would have been treated with great respect and would have passed through high school with greater ease for him and for us. But Catholic Central offered the possibility for Alan to remain in a mainstream educational program, where he could compete with the best-of-the-best academically and grow from that challenge.

Alan's excitement for new knowledge and friends fueled his passion to achieve beyond his physical weakness. He often appeared lethargic on Sunday nights but would wake on Monday mornings with the energy of ten strong men. No matter how bad he felt physically, as soon as he entered the school, a transformation took over that made him stronger and more determined.

A Parent's Thoughts

Look for the different choices available when facing a problem. One option often exists that feels right but may not be viewed initially as the most practical. This choice of the heart often provides the most amazing results.

Insight 4

Look and listen for the angels who enter our lives; they are daily miracles.

In 1997, the Detroit Red Wings won the Stanley Cup, hockey's greatest trophy. Alan and his brother, Andy, called me the morning of the victory parade and pleaded with me to take them. The Red Wings had been a major influence in their lives that year. Alan and Andy slept in their Red Wings shirts every night during the playoffs, they had purchased player cards of their favorite Red Wings, and their school even had Red Wings jerseys hanging from the ceiling rafters of the school. The parade began at noon, yet they called me at 10:00 a.m. I knew I had to take them, but how could I get Alan close enough to see the parade when the radio said nearly one million people were already downtown?

Alan had just begun using a manual wheelchair that year and I was still learning the steps I needed to follow when taking him places. Parking needed to be close to the event so I could push the chair without getting tired. I needed to leave ample time to arrive at events so I could get close and avoid having to make our way through a large crowd. This parade went against all of these precautions. It was already too late to get close parking to the parade. Yet in spite of this, I decided to try.

Good fortune rode with me that morning. I knew the back streets of Detroit very well, having learned from my father, who took great pride in knowing multiple ways to get in and out of various cities. I maneuvered quickly into town. Parking proved easy. I drove past what looked like a full parking lot. A tall, thin man wearing all red jumped out in front of my van and waved me into the lot. He had one slot left, right in front of the exit. Perfect. I could get Alan out easily.

The difficult part would be getting him close enough to the parade so he could see. With one-million-plus Red Wings fans along the one-and-a-half-mile parade route, I needed all the strength I could gather to take on this crowd. The easy parking gave me renewed energy even though the temperature was 88°F.

Gwen and I kept walking in the hope of finding an opening in the crowd. I left Gwen with the boys and headed toward a spot where a few trees were providing shade. I wanted to see if we could get Alan under one of them. No luck—completely full. I turned to find Gwen and the boys but could not see them. When I finally caught sight of Gwen, she was walking quickly behind a man who was parting the crowd as he walked in order to make room for Alan.

"What is going on?" I asked.

"This guy just came up to me and asked if we needed a spot for Alan. He said his family had arrived around 1:00 a.m. to get a curbside view. He asked that we join him."

This special man was a dentist in the Detroit area. He not only placed Alan on the curb, under the shade of a tent, but offered all of us drinks and snacks. He never asked much detail about Alan. We sat right where the Red Wings players walked and were able to get autographs from many of the players. Alan's dream was fulfilled thanks to the efforts of a willing "angel" in the crowd.

◊　◊　◊

There is a pattern of this occurring over the years. Family, friends, and strangers come seemingly out of nowhere to help, and just at the right moment. I learned over time to listen carefully to the comments made by these folks. Often they say something that triggers ideas that end up helping Alan.

◊　◊　◊

My cousin Margie sent an e-mail to me at work when Alan had just started using the wheelchair. She was recovering from an injury caused by a tube that had been inserted into her throat during surgery. She had been researching vitamins and minerals that could help her regain energy and strength. She found a vitamin for Alan. Her note gave me the idea to do my own research into what might help Alan regain his stamina.

Several weeks after that, a friend stopped me in the parking lot at school. He looked more excited than usual. He had seen Alan a few days earlier and noted that Alan had looked weaker. This bothered him so much that he offered to give Alan his appointment with a nutrition specialist who worked with local sports teams. This doctor specialized in strength conditioning to prevent disease. Normally I would have been skeptical of this idea, but my recent exchange of notes with Margie had prepared me to take this offer seriously.

Our first visit with this doctor proved revealing. He immediately told us that Alan's body needed a lot more nutrition. His tests revealed low protein and a high level of toxins in his blood. He placed Alan on a regimen of vitamins and minerals that cost over $200. I had doubts and almost did not buy the supplements.

In just a short period of time, the results of him taking the supplements were amazing. Alan's energy and stamina grew stronger, and the color of his cheeks went from pale white to rosy. He had energy from 7:00 a.m. to 9:00 p.m., going to school all day and then doing homework in the evening. Alan's spirit seemed lighter, and he looked happier and appeared calmer. I could have missed this chance to help Alan if I had ignored the seemingly unconnected messages that came my way from people like my cousin Margie and the friend at school.

I mentioned these coincidences one day to a lady, Camille, whom I met at a local college. I was attending a lecture series on how to motivate employees in the workplace. This particular lecture was about learning to listen to others and use what they say to build a communication path with more and more people. I gave her a quick recap of what occurred regarding Alan and the nutritional supplements. When I mentioned the *coincidence* of events that had led me to the doctor, she immediately interrupted and stressed very emphatically that the coincidences were not really random. She stressed that connections between people and ideas continuously occur and that we need to pay attention. People enter our lives for a purpose, often at the right moment to provide a link to something else or to deliver a message.

Throughout her class, Camille kept referring to my story. A few years earlier I probably would have concluded that

Camille was just another one of "those spiritualists" wanting to make any event appear mysterious. But recent events with Alan stopped me from being negative. I hung on every word, moving from listening to Camille to getting caught up in my own thoughts, trying to look back on events that had connections. And then I remembered one.

We had just moved from our historic neighborhood to a newer neighborhood and a home with a backyard three times the size of what we had had in Dearborn. Although our new home was much newer than the 1919 home we just moved from, the city we moved to—Plymouth, Michigan— looked like an old New England town.

The new neighborhood was much quieter. In Dearborn, we had lived across the street from train tracks. Amtrak trains mainly used these tracks. Even though the trains ran only twice a day, they were noisy and the rooms in the house shook from the rumble of the tracks. Michigan Avenue ran just beyond the tracks. The noise from that road added to the noise level and to the air pollution.

In Plymouth, we had nearly the opposite conditions. Initially, we could not hear anything in the way of traffic noise. However, after several weeks of relative silence and not having to filter out so much background noise, we began to notice the faint sounds of traffic and an occasional train whistle in the distance. We were shocked at how much noise we had filtered out while we lived in the busy city of Dearborn. It made us wonder what else we filtered out in a given day, just to keep our lives simpler and more manageable.

One day, Gwen had a great story to tell me when I came home from work. She had taken the boys to the Plymouth library and had met another mother there who had two sons. It was a chance meeting that occurred just as Gwen, Alan, and Andy left the library. This mom's kids both had muscular dystrophy. They did not look like it at first since they were younger, but they did fall a lot, much like Alan. Gwen was so excited to have found a friend with very similar problems.

The father of these boys worked, like me, at Ford Motor Company. Gwen thought I should send him an e-mail to introduce myself and find out what he might be like. One night we met at the local park to let the boys play together and share our struggles and worries. Gwen and I talked about our recent move to Plymouth. We described the home we had left in Dearborn and how we had reworked the entire place, restoring the original beauty and adding a family room and bedroom to make the home more functional for today's lifestyles.

I had just finished explaining how I had moved the kitchen doorway to enhance the dining room space when Bruce, the father of the twin boys, yelled, "Hold on a minute! Are you talking about the home in West Dearborn within the Ford Historic Home District?"

"Yes."

"The house on the corner with train tracks across the street?"

"Yes."

"The house with a new addition in the back that has a flower bed on the second floor just outside the bedroom window?"

"Yes."

"We looked at that house a year ago and almost bought it. The boys had begun falling a lot that year, so we decided not to buy your home. Too many stairs to climb."

What a coincidence. Then I could hear Camille's voice

claiming that there is no such thing as a coincidence. In that case, the similarities of our families were remarkable.

Bruce and Annette, it turned out, were more connected to the muscular dystrophy organization than we were. They were more experienced in pursuing the options available for their sons. They became our connection to an organization of people who could help Alan on his journey of perseverance over illness. Doctors with insight into Alan's disease became accessible to us. Events such as Halloween parties for dystrophy kids, Christmas parties, a wheelchair hockey league, and summer camps became opportunities for Alan to socialize without being the "different one" in a wheelchair.

This "coincidental" encounter with Bruce and Annette helped open up several significant experiences for Alan. For instance, the Muscular Dystrophy Association sponsors a summer camp. Gwen and I had not liked the idea of our little boy going off for one week to a camp with kids that looked more physically ill than he did. We feared Alan would see himself too much as a disabled kid and not as a mainstream kid with physical problems. We also feared for his care.

We developed a "high alert" mentality and were constantly monitoring his needs. To let him go for one week, even though it offered us a much-deserved break, produced a big sense of insecurity over who could take better care of Alan than Gwen and I.

While agonizing over the pros and cons of Alan going to camp, we met the camp director. Julie just loved the children, spending a nearly sleepless week watching over her "friends." The older kids were treated like big sisters and brothers. Julie handled the younger kids as if she were their mother.

Julie applied no pressure. She just gave us details about how many doctors volunteered their time to spend the week with the children. "More doctors than a typical hospital" was how Julie portrayed the camp.

Alan went to camp the year he entered fourth grade. We had to drive two-and-a-half hours on Father's Day to the camp on Lake Huron. I was still not convinced that this camp would be right. At that time he walked with braces and knee pads. We brought all of Alan's favorite blankets, stuffed animals, and handheld electronic games. My heart ached to see the small cabin with all those kids crammed into it. The camp rule was one aide per child, with the aide sleeping next to the child. Gwen and I were just about to leave when Tim, the cabin "parent," came in.

He looked like he could be a younger brother of mine. He quickly glanced over the crowd in the cabin, assessing who needed what. He walked over to Alan and introduced himself. He spotted the box of sports cards on Alan's bed.

"Those your cards?"

"I have cards for baseball, football, hockey, and basketball," Alan said.

"We will be best buddies this week, Al. I love talking sports."

Alan's face glowed with that "rearview mirror" look of expectation and anticipation. Once I saw that look, I knew camp would be great. He had totally forgotten we were there, getting into small conversations with other kids. In Alan's mind, he had already made the break from us. Gwen and I needed to do the same. We kissed him goodbye and left with tears in our eyes.

The angel at camp turned out to be Tim. His generosity and enthusiasm opened up a new world for Alan, filling him with a desire to grow up and be like the role model Tim was to him. Tim went to Notre Dame University and planned to be a doctor. Alan suddenly became very interested in colleges and began setting goals to attend. If not for Tim, I am not sure Alan would have developed such a strong passion for university life.

The special people who came into our lives at just the right moment brought with them a positive energy. This energy fueled our desires for adventure, inspired fresh new goals to achieve, and opened up our sense of what is possible. Without these people, I do not believe Alan could have achieved what he did. They entered our lives in what seemed to be coincidental moments. Being receptive to these moments led to more and more positive "coincidences."

Alan with Jerry Rice, 2010 Hall of Fame football player, at a New York Knicks basketball game he attended through Make-A-Wish in 2002.

Soon Alan's life was filled with such a variety of people and experiences that he began to aspire for things beyond what would normally be expected from a kid in his physical condition. He started to live beyond himself and his physical problems. Each person who entered his life delivered a message, an activity, an idea, or a friendship that opened up new possibilities for him.

A Parent's Thoughts

Look back upon recent events and identify those seemingly random people who enter your life. Do they bring a message, help solve a problem? Follow these connections. By doing this, you will make yourself more aware and open to the world and what it has to offer.

54

The Angels Make Their Move—
Deciding to Live

2007

This morning, a quiet Sunday in the hospital, offered a brief reprieve from the pressures of trying to get Alan well. I read my paper. Alan looked peaceful. I vowed not to bring up the need for Alan to work harder at pulling out the mucus. The doctors were about to conclude that Alan could no longer breathe on his own without a full-time ventilator.

That decision, however, would be delayed for another day. The calm felt good. No primary doctor visits today. Alan asked me to find a soccer game on TV. This was the first time since he had entered the hospital that he had shown interest in anything, including his much-loved sports teams.

We found a U.S. match. I do not care much for soccer, so I continued to read the paper.

"Oh, soccer. I just love the sport."

I looked up from my paper. A soft-spoken man with a Bible in his hand stood at the foot of Alan's bed. He did not look at Alan or at me but was watching the game.

"Back in my homeland, soccer was all we had. My brother and I waited several years to finally get our own ball. I found God in my heart as I played soccer."

I remained silent. Alan beamed with a big smile that I had not seen for many weeks. He had been trying to convince me to give soccer a chance, and our visitor said what Alan would have said if he had been able.

"Can we say a prayer together?"

"Certainly," I said.

"Hail Mary, full of Grace, the Lord is with thee. Blessed art thou amongst women and blessed is the fruit of thy womb, Jesus. Holy Mary, Mother of God, pray for us sinners now and at the hour of our death. Amen. Please send the healing power of God to our brother. Amen."

I watched Alan. His eyes looked sparkly blue again. A warm smile cut across the tense muscles in his face and the tube in his mouth looked insignificant for a moment.

Our visitor, who never told me his name, was a visiting priest from Africa. He touched Alan's hands and face, looked at me, and said, "Now that is a look of healing."

He left. Five minutes later, Alan grunted to get my attention. Using the letter board, he spelled "Get the nurse."

Alan wanted to be taken off the respirator to test his strength, which the doctors had been pressing him to do all week.

Alan stayed off the machine for two hours. It was an amazing change in events. The doctors and nurses were suddenly buzzing with energy, offering to assist in other exercises that could get him off the machines and back home. I marveled at how one spark of love and hope, ignited by the African priest, had set off a chain of positive energy and feeling.

Alan showed a will to fight for his life and for future independence. But his fight seemed to peak a few days later and then remain stagnant. He could not get beyond two hours off the machine. The doctors became skeptical about Alan's ability to survive without the ventilator.

On Sunday one week later, the priest returned. He walked in as before, noticed soccer on the TV, and began to talk about his childhood.

"I found God while playing soccer. I have this amazing gift to be able to look into a person's eyes and see if they have the will to win, the power to believe. On the soccer field, I could tell if my opponent had the will to win. I often used this ability to take advantage of the weaker members of the opposing team. I would tell my teammates to focus upon the players with the weak will. Looking into another person's eyes rarely failed me in figuring out whether they were strong or weak.

"One day, God told me to use this ability for a better purpose—to help weaker people believe instead of taking advantage of their weakened condition. So here I am, a priest at the University of Michigan Hospital, looking for ways to strengthen the will to believe and live. May we pray together?"

After the prayer, he looked into my eyes like no one ever had. He said again, "I have the power to understand a person through their eyes."

He then looked at Alan, touched his head, and said a silent prayer. I looked into Alan's eyes and saw the return of the radiant blue. Alan smiled as he had the previous Sunday.

The priest looked at me and said, "Now that is the look of healing. I must go now. Take care, Alan."

And just like that he was gone.

As had happened the week before, ten minutes after the priest left the room, Alan asked for the nurse to come. This time Alan stayed off the breathing machine for eight hours. His determination was back, stronger than ever.

Unfortunately, Alan's will to get better was not enough. He took charge every day now, attempting to beat his previous day's time off of the machine, but the mucus would not go away. Even though Alan had the strength to wean himself off the machinery, the tube down his throat could not be removed until all of the fluid in his lungs had been pulled out.

A week after the second visit from the soccer priest, the tube was still in his throat. On the Wednesday morning of that week, the lead doctor wanted to talk.

"Alan," he said, "I see only a ten percent hope that we can pull the tube out and that you will be able to breathe on your own again. I believe you need to be placed on a permanent ventilator. We can schedule a time for Friday to perform the procedure."

Alan looked terrified. I felt powerless. The nightmare continued to unfold. Gwen asked if the ventilator would change Alan's ability to talk.

"We will be cutting a hole in the trachea and inserting a tube adaptor. The vocal chords will not be touched, but the flow around the vocal chords will change. This will change Alan's voice and could prevent him from speaking freely."

Alan's inability to speak would take away the only means of communication he had. What kind of life would he have? Could he continue his studies?

"Alan, why don't you discuss this with your mom and dad? I will come back in a while."

When everyone left the room, Alan fixed his eyes upon me. That same "So, what do you think, Dad?" look covered his face, that look he had when we sat in the dining room on that Saturday morning when he was three years old. I had no idea what to say. I'd sat with him for several weeks now and watched him struggle to get better. Clearly he'd hit a wall in his recovery since we had not seen progress for several days.

Alan signaled for me to grab the alphabet pad. Slowly he spelled out, "So what is the plan, Dad?"

Oh my God. What a thing to decide. My beautiful son's future seemed to depend upon my thoughts. I wanted his future to be full of achievements, like his interest in writing articles about politics and sports. But I had no idea how to get there. I feared the tracheotomy would take away his potential. I struggled for words.

I finally said, "Alan, let's wait a few more days to decide. In the meantime, you need to keep working hard to get the fluids out."

I had a strong feeling in my gut that a few more days could make a difference, giving us more choices. But I had no clue what to do next.

Just as I finished talking to Alan, a voice on my right said, "That's right, Dad, I have seen this before. I have a plan, Al. If you are willing to work with me today, I believe we can rid you of these fluids."

I looked over and saw a young man with short black hair, a youthful face that could make him my son, and muscles bulging from his forearms. He looked right at Alan, not taking his eyes off him until he had gotten a nod of agreement to begin working hard.

"Who are you?" I asked.

"I am Alan's nurse today."

We had been there for three weeks and I never had seen this young man before.

"I will be with Alan for twelve hours. You go home, Dad, and get some sleep. I have a plan."

No one had come in over the previous three weeks with a plan. He immediately snapped into action. Before I could leave, he had lifted Alan off the bed and placed him in a new position. He was trying to loosen the fluids by moving him around.

"Keep working with me, Al," he was saying as I left the room.

Insight 5

Live your dreams, not your troubles.

Alan achieves beyond expectations because he does not see limitations for himself. He lives for his dreams and goals, never looking back. Alan's ambitions do not differ from those of physically healthy people. He believes a little technology and a bit of help from a friend can overcome any obstacle.

His freshman year at Catholic Central brought with it many opportunities for developing skills. Chess Club, Debate Team, and French Club all looked interesting. But the one team he wanted to try most was called Quiz Bowl Team.

Quiz Bowl competitions test a participant's knowledge of facts related to history, politics, math, science, English, and possibly sports. The CC team had ranked number one in the nation for several years. Eligibility requirements for the freshman squad meant that the kids had to participate in practice rounds with the teacher for several weeks. Kids who performed well were asked to stay.

The first sessions were held in early August on Tuesday evenings. Just showing up several weeks before school officially began to participate in practice rounds gave these kids an advantage over those who showed up after school started. Two teams, consisting of three kids per team, would huddle around a large button connected by a wire to a scoreboard. Hitting the button first gave that team a chance to answer the question. If the team was correct, they were given a point. If they were incorrect in their answer, the opposing team had a chance to answer. If the opposing team answered correctly, then they received a point and the lead for the next question.

I took Alan to the first few summer sessions to observe. Clearly Alan had the knowledge and quickness of response to compete. What he could not do was hit the button. The teacher of this freshman team did not know how to handle this situation. Rather than trying to figure out a solution, she chose to ignore him. He never had a chance to be with a team until, at the end of one session, several boys took it upon themselves to team up with Alan. They worked out a routine where they watched Alan's eyes when a question was asked. If Alan nodded his head, they hit the button. The team won as many as they lost that day, with Alan contributing significantly to the wins. It was difficult to tell if that slight delay from when Alan nodded his head to when the other kid hit the button impacted their chances to get the first response. It took the boys' initiative to figure out a method for Alan to participate, but the teacher still looked uneasy with the arrangement.

Alan made the team and traveled from one tournament to another. The freshman team had a winning record going into a school-sponsored state competition on a Saturday in January. Alan felt good about himself; the Quiz Bowl team was satisfying his need to compete and sharpen his skills. However, this day of competition turned sour quickly.

I had not worried about the tournament in terms of logistics since it was at Alan's high school. However, when Gwen and Alan arrived, the teacher/coach walked up to

Alan and said the room that they were competing in did not have easy access for a wheelchair. She suggested they just wait on the main floor until it was over. This crushed Alan. Several other parents heard what had happened and came right over to offer ideas on what to do. Together, Gwen and the moms found a way to get Alan inside the room by taking him outside and around the building to a lower-level door. The teacher looked stunned when Alan entered the room and took his place with the team.

After the round, Gwen found the leader of the competition, who was from the University of Michigan. He told Gwen that Alan's team had never requested that the room be changed to accommodate him and that he would have changed to another room if he had known about the need.

It turned out that the teacher/coach had deliberately not requested a new room to accommodate Alan. She wanted to discourage him from participating and hoped this event would do so. She had not felt comfortable dealing with his needs and hoped he would just go away. To her, winning meant more than giving Alan a chance to participate. She feared that the split-second delay between Alan's head nod and his team member hitting the button would hurt the team's chances of winning.

Alan felt rejected due to his physical condition. All other facets of school life were working very well, but this one event threatened the whole. To Alan's credit, his response to the rejection was to prove wrong those who believed he could not compete alongside the "normal" kids.

One week following the Quiz Bowl incident, Alan came home and declared his participation in the school's writing contest. He wanted to arrive early to the Saturday morning event and asked that Gwen or I go with him to write what he dictated.

I have terrible handwriting, so Gwen and Alan left for the writing contest that morning, uncertain about how Alan's needs would be accommodated. When they arrived, the head of the school's English department greeted them. He had already worked out a plan to help Alan participate. He had heard about the Quiz Bowl problem and was determined not to let that occur with his event.

Although hurting from the Quiz Bowl rejection, Alan remained positive and determined to write well. No preparation was required. Each student could choose one of five statements made by historical figures. They were to respond to the statement, agreeing or disagreeing, with examples to justify their position.

Alan finished on time. He refused to take any extra time the instructor was offering to accommodate his physical restrictions. He wanted to make the point that he could participate and win within the same constraints as others. He had to work faster and harder than the others, dictating all of his outlines and final drafts. For Alan, this was his moment to respond and "get back" at those who had doubted or resented him.

Alan won freshman honors and came in fifth overall in the school. However, fifth place was not good enough for Alan. He went on to win first place overall two years later and became the editor-in-chief of the school newspaper.

In spite of these accomplishments, Alan began to feel left behind when his friends started playing sports for the high school. Although his friends were still around, he could not share in the experience of competition.

Alan loves sports. He reads all the sport publications and magazines. He belongs to several sports fantasy leagues—bas-

ketball, football, baseball, and hockey. He owns an impressive sports card collection. He naturally attracts a crowd of dads at events when he begins to share his very informed opinions on the latest sports topics. He takes a stand and defends his opinions well with facts that few know.

One day, Alan asked me to take him to a wheelchair hockey tryout practice session—at camp he had played floor hockey and loved it. His camp friends were playing in an organized league dedicated to kids in wheelchairs and one of them had called looking for a few new players. They played on a basketball court, using a plastic ball for a puck. Players ranged in ability from those with good hand and arm strength, riding manual wheelchairs, to kids who had to tie their hockey sticks to their motorized wheelchairs because they did not have the arm strength to control them.

Alan joined a team called the Hornets. He would be their goalie.

Alan playing goalie in wheelchair hockey league, 2005.

Early in the season, the Hornets played the reigning champions. This team had several strong kids who could quickly maneuver the ball down the court, weaving their manual chairs in and around the other wheelchairs. One particular player, Tony, had a metallic green wheelchair, its front wheels slanted inward to provide a better grip for faster maneuvers. Tony did not seem to think much of Alan at first.

Alan had the biggest smile before the game. But when the ball/puck was dropped and play began, he looked fierce. Patrick Roy, a very successful goalie in the National Hockey League, had been Alan's hockey idol for many years. Alan had studied Roy's moves and watched how he anticipated shots and was always in the right place to stop the puck. Now I could see Alan studying the opponents and their moves, looking for their tendencies and strengths, just like Roy.

Tony came down the court early in the first period, breaking away from the crowd of players at center court. He shifted the ball from one side to the other, trying to get Alan to commit a movement one way or another. But Alan remained steady, keeping his chair square with the angle Tony had been coming from. Tony looked baffled as he got closer. He finally committed to the front of Alan, and Alan moved his chair forward enough to cut off any angle to the net. Tony did not take a shot. He looked back at Alan as if to say, "Who is this new kid?"

At the next opportunity, Tony had a plan. He shot toward Alan from a distance, with the intention of picking up the rebound and getting a second shot. He shot, and Alan deflected the ball in the opposite direction from where Tony was. Again foiled, Tony started to get angry. I became concerned, not wanting to see Alan get hurt.

Alan's captain saw the emerging conflict and decided to double-team the defense against Tony to stop him from getting easy shots. Knowing this, Alan focused on the second goal-shooter on the team, trying to anticipate his moves. Throughout the entire game, Alan never once smiled. He kept a strong, fierce look on his face.

Clearly this "team of champions" was not accustomed to being scoreless. In the final minute of play, they charged the net in full force. One shot after another bounced off Alan's chair. Never once did Alan flinch. The Hornets' parents began to count down the seconds, just praying nothing would slip past Alan's chair. Finally, the buzzer sounded. A moment later, the ball slid past Alan's chair and into the goal. The champions were so focused on scoring that they never heard the buzzer and began to celebrate as if they had tied the game. In fact, they had lost their first game in two years, and Alan had a shutout in his first game.

The champions protested everything, saying Alan's chair was too low and that the backpack hanging from the rear of the chair was somehow "unfair." But it did not matter—they had lost and the Hornets had won. Alan felt exhausted. During the ride home, he had that tired yet excited look. On Monday he would be able to share his own sports competition story, telling his friends how he had felt and what great moves he had made. As always, Alan had found a way to go beyond his circumstances and enjoy the same pleasures as kids who did not have physical challenges.

◇ ◇ ◇

Tuesday, October 8, 2003, several days following his hockey success, Alan's life took a dark turn. He came home from school feeling tired and short of breath. Around five o'clock in the afternoon, he began to cough. Alan had severe curvature of the spine, and because of that, he had less lung capacity than most. The coughing caused him to have even shorter breath. Gwen, Andy, and his new sister, Lili, took Alan to the emergency room, where he was immediately diagnosed as having a minor case of bronchitis. The X-rays looked clear, but he was kept overnight for observation.

I stayed the night, sitting in an office-type chair, my feet propped up on another stiff chair. Neither of us got much sleep. The doctors, a team of four, were conducting tests, and at around six o'clock in the morning they concluded Alan had pneumonia. A portion of his lungs, hard to see on the X-rays, contained built-up fluid that needed to come out. Alan was admitted to a room on the fifth floor of the Children's Hospital in Ann Arbor. The doctors started Alan on a breathing treatment designed to pull the fluid out of his lungs. Alan held a plastic pipe-like tube in his mouth while a machine pumped gas into his lungs to penetrate the mucus and break it up.

Alan could not sleep after the first night of this treatment. I sat with him talking about sports and politics. Alan had begun reading political websites in order to better understand the upcoming presidential election. We talked for hours, but I finally told him to rest. The respiratory therapist came in to hook him up to a BiPAP machine, which pushed air into Alan's lungs while he slept. The machine pushed air only when it sensed a need. Attached to Alan's finger was a monitor for his heart rate and the oxygen count in his blood. The nurse told me to keep an eye on the oxygen level, for a drop in this could cause critical consequences.

Alan fell asleep. I sat down right next to him. I focused on the beeps and kept an eye on the oxygen level count. Alan looked peaceful, but then, just as if someone had flipped a switch, panic was everywhere. His oxygen level dropped below the required level and would not come back up. The nurse rushed in and immediately called for a code blue, meaning emergency condition. Alan was talking to me; he looked good, but he was nervous. I started rubbing his arm, and naturally he calmed down to the point where the oxygen level began to rise. Another nurse, standing next to me, saw this as well. We brushed his hair and kept rubbing his arm until he fully recovered the oxygen level.

One minute after he stabilized, a team of very young physicians came running into the room, ready to cut him open and insert a tube for a respirator. I stopped them with a wave of my hand. They had an almost crazed look in their eyes, which scared me.

"Who are you?" they shouted.

"I am Alan's dad. He has settled down. His oxygen level is back up. He is resting now. Let's leave him alone."

They did not like my saying this, but the nurse who had helped me all along confirmed what I said. I knew they had me labeled as a troublesome parent, but they left, warning me that he could have difficulty recovering again if we did not hook him up to a ventilator.

Several days before, Gwen and I had had a big discussion with the doctors. They had advocated hooking Alan up to a ventilator system, meaning Alan would have a tube in his throat permanently, impeding his speaking ability and his mobility. Knowing Alan's dream to be a politician and writer, and his strong will to succeed, we refused to grant permission. Alan looked good and was in high spirits. I was more determined than ever to give Alan every conceivable chance to recover without this machine.

Alan slept well that night. In the morning, I left for work and Gwen came to be with Alan during the day. He ate plenty of food that morning and looked relaxed. A doctor we had not seen before visited Alan. She had received word from the night-shift doctors about the incident that had occurred during the night. I could detect that she had already concluded Alan needed a respirator and that it would be only a matter of time before everyone came to the same conclusion.

Several days later, Alan became so frightened about a procedure they wanted to do on him that he started to panic. His breathing became shallow and his oxygen level fell again. Gwen called me at work and said, "Get here fast. Alan needs you."

I had been conducting a seminar at work, but I turned the seminar over to my assistant and ran out. Tears flowed from my eyes. What had gone wrong? When I got to Alan's room, he looked calm, but his oxygen level continued to waver. Doctors were again stressing the need to hook him up to a ventilator. Gwen had stopped them, telling them that Alan's dad was on the way. Gwen and I comforted him by rubbing his arms and telling him he would be fine.

I tried something new. I began telling him about a new report I had heard on National Public Radio. Almost in an instant, this bit of news caught Alan's attention. Gwen and I could not believe what we saw. Alan's breathing got stronger, his oxygen level went up and stayed up, and his eyes were wide open with a look of excitement. He wanted to talk politics with me. The doctors went away and Alan talked the rest of the afternoon with us. The doctors did place him in intensive care that evening to give him more one-on-one care and treatment.

Alan remained stable for days but never seemed to grow stronger. Friends and neighbors visited and we watched baseball playoffs on TV.

One day, a good friend of mine from work visited Alan. Greg loved politics and was always ready for a good discussion. When he entered the room, Greg saw the book *Lies and the Lying Liars Who Tell Them* by Al Franken on the table by Alan's bed. Greg is a Republican at heart. He asked Alan if he had been reading it and then suggested, "You'd better turn up the oxygen for this boy. His judgment appears impaired."

This brought a smile to Alan's face; he loved a good discussion. While the two of them began debating ideas, I grabbed a chair and sat back to watch. As I listened to this debate, I kept an eye on the hospital monitors. Alan's oxygen level and other indicators reached positive levels I had not seen before. While Greg and Alan were debating politics, Alan made the progress we had been praying for. That evening, the chief doctor of respiratory care visited for the first time. He, too, spotted the book and started asking Alan about it. Again, Alan's condition improved. The doctor took notes and kept the discussion going. When he left, he pulled me aside and said, "This is some son you have. He will be just fine."

Alan left the hospital a few days later with no ventilator. He actually looked fresher and stronger than before. We talked politics and sports all the way home. The way Alan was able to project himself beyond his immediate physical condition and look toward where he wanted to be symbolized the way he always handled situations. Alan drew strength from anticipating new goals and projects. His plan for attending college and his love for sports and politics kept him from dwelling on his physical problems and propelled him toward new heights.

A Parent's Thoughts

Dr. Wayne Dyer, in his book *Inspiration: Your Ultimate Calling* (pg 30), states,

"We become what we think about."

Watching Alan over the years, I believe I understand what Dr. Dyer means. When Alan sees himself as strong, capable of attending school, and skilled in the art of writing and debate, he literally transcends his physical problems at the moment, gaining strength and forging on with a determination few healthy men his age have. Alan truly uses his mind to impact his life. He can turn a bad moment into a positive one by altering what he focuses on, shifting from the pain and frustration to the possibilities of achievement.

Insight 6

Avoid isolation, the silent enemy.

Alan's disease manifested slowly at first; he walked all through sixth grade. Each year, however, his walking became more and more tenuous. By fifth grade he wore knee pads all of the time to protect him from frequent falls.

The kids at school reacted in various ways to Alan's changing physical condition. The majority of the kids began to shy away from him. Only two boys and one girl remained his close friends during the remainder of his grade school years.

Our tendency to isolate those who are different certainly harms the person who is different. Alan became resentful and angry toward those who suddenly acted as if they had never known him. Many parents tried to explain to me that their kids simply did not know how to react or what to say or do. Knowing the parents as I did, I believed them. For the most part, their kids did not intend to be mean; they felt awkward around Alan and did not know how to handle it.

In the years to come, most of these kids and parents stepped forward in acts of kindness and love. Although these one-time acts were beautiful when they happened, the day-to-day actions of acceptance were the acts Alan needed most.

◇　◇　◇

Daily acceptance goes beyond the "feel good" idea: it is Alan needing to feel that he is like everyone else. Alan wants to hear the anticipation of great things for him from his family and friends such as, "When you grow up, you will become a great scientist (or author, etc.)." Alan does not need or want pity. He instead yearns for expectations from society that he do his best and become a difference-maker.

◇   ◇   ◇

I made sure Alan had a chance to attend all of the after-school events. I often took time off from work to help him into people's homes for parties or to go with him to the movies with his friends. I would sit in the last row so he could sit up front with his friends and feel a bit of independence. This effort worked for awhile and Alan did not feel isolated. But I also could see how awkward it would become going forward and that it would begin to have an opposite impact, making Alan feel more isolated because his dad needed to be with him.

Family parties started to bring out the best in Alan. As his physical condition worsened, he enjoyed the birthday parties and holiday events more and more. Usually pre-teens and young teenagers will reject such events, but Alan responded the opposite way. At family parties, relatives would spend time talking with him and included him in all of their discussions. At these events, he felt the wheelchair had no bearing on how he was treated. When my brother, Ron, began to challenge Alan on his views regarding politics, sports, or films, Alan gained self-confidence and felt as if his opinion mattered and was significant. The more the family interacted with him in a normal way, not fearing they would hurt his feelings or insult him with a comment, the more Alan felt accepted.

In my teenage years, I rejected all family events. I slowly worked to separate myself from all previous familial associations. I wanted to become something different from my parents and relatives. I needed to explore new ideas and new career options beyond the expectations of my family. My extended family consists of hard-working people of Polish heritage. They live their lives for the children. The neighbors I grew up around worked in factories or owned small businesses. They loved weddings, other family parties, and sports. They drank beer in excess at parties and ate heartily. Many died young. Few marriages ended in divorce. This environment did provide a sense of security, but I also sensed a feeling of depression and dullness permeating the landscape. I wanted to find a different lifestyle.

I stopped going to family events. My father passed away. I was fifteen years old and resented him for leaving me. I became sick of the cycle of death and what I perceived as mediocrity in the lives around me. I looked for a new life among my friends in college.

I attended film festivals and visited New York, Toronto, and Chicago to experience the energy of large cities. I found books in little hideaway bookstores in my travels. I started reading authors like Sartre and Camus and attended dinners with my college professors, discussing abstract ideas like free will and punishment, existentialism, relativity, and crime and punishment.

One Friday evening in October, I sat in the backyard of the home of my professor of philosophy. Several other students and friends were there. We ate spaghetti while sitting under a large apple tree. A visiting professor delivered a summary of his new book and wanted some serious feedback. I felt proud to be there, expecting to share my opinions with these highly educated people. I thought I had finally made the break from my past, finding a new existence.

Besides staying physically away from many family and old friends, I created an emotional shield as well. When I did attend birthday parties and holiday events, I kept telling myself that I was not like them and I always looked for ways to separate myself from the rest. I would spend my time at parties either playing with my niece and nephew or entering into debates with the adults, relishing the opposing view to test my skills and knowledge and to see how they would respond.

During my college years, I took a year off from school to "find myself." For one year, I lived between the cracks of society. With no job, no school to attend, and no social contact with most family members, I relished the feeling of almost nonexistence. Fittingly, I read many books about existential psychology, which emphasized the duality between being and nothingness. I wanted to push the limits of nothingness without reaching despair. By doing this, I found I was able to go through a cleansing process, giving me a clean break from my past and the traditional expectations for a young man from my background. I believed that I had choices, and this began to overwhelm me. Choice provides an opportunity to act.

My sister expected me to be socially involved with family and friends. Keeping a scorecard—tracking how much time and money we gave to family members and how often the act was returned in kind stood out as her prime social motivation. Family politics really mattered to her. My brother expected me to follow a non-creative path in life, in contrast to his perceived view of himself as the creative guru of the family. Former teachers expected me to go off and make lots of money and be influential. These expectations functioned as weights upon my soul.

For one year, I did not satisfy anyone's expectations. However, living without purpose, goals, and expectations started to drive me insane. I tried hard to resist these feelings and enjoy my "nothing" life. However, my frustration continued to grow.

One day, a professor friend called and asked if I would help him with a theater production he was working on. The play, *The Importance of Being Ernest*, required many stage props, like chairs, tables, and lamps. Several major scene changes were written into the script. My friend asked me to find the furniture and props from theater companies in the area. He also wanted me to be the stage manager, which meant I had to direct the non-acting people on what to do during scene changes. I jumped at this chance to get involved again in life, particularly involved with creative people who defied the norm of the people I had grown up with.

Theater people can be very emotional. Some are rather bizarre in their view of life. Several were extremely nervous and concerned about their appearance. Two young ladies were extremely beautiful and knew it. Yet in spite of the eccentricities and anxieties of this group, they had a great ability to accept all within their ranks. Everyone was accepted without question and all were part of a common goal: to create.

I had grown up in an environment where people in theater were viewed as weird, impractical, and to be avoided. Because of this, I enjoyed the theater experience more than if I had been taught to appreciate it. These people were brilliant in their ideas and insights. They never won academic awards in school and were generally considered average and a bit odd by most. Yet their thoughts were fresh and full of life, much like children at play. They generally lived for the moment at hand. Many avoided with a passion anything having to do with commercialism and the need to be successful in the eyes of society. Their approach opened my eyes to a new view of my own existence, even justifying what I had been trying to do personally. For once, I actually experienced what the possibilities could be with an alternative view of life.

I began to respect my creative instincts. My new friends saw the creativity within me, even if I had not yet seen it for myself. They encouraged me to write and draw. They loved hearing about the books on philosophy I had read. For that brief moment in my life, I felt totally accepted and as if I were an artist. The self-doubt within me disappeared. Several of my ideas were incorporated into the production. Those ideas worked very well, encouraging me further to trust in my skills.

Looking back after twenty years, I can see how that time in my life with the people in theater prepared me for my trials with Alan. These friends showed me the importance of being involved with others. My theater friends' unconditional respect for talents they saw within me, which I did not see, taught me how to be an active participant in life and not give up ideas and plans that most would view as unnecessary and frivolous. The biggest lesson was that I did need others to motivate me toward things that might otherwise have appeared unattainable. Learning to trust others also became a lesson learned. Only in an environment of trust can ideas blossom and become realities. These lessons prepared me well as a guide to helping Alan achieve his ambitions.

I knew from my own journey that I needed to keep Alan from feeling isolated. He needed to believe that he had chances to meet people, like I had had, who would see beyond his physical limits and identify his talents and ability to achieve great things. What I never expected was how my past, the people and institutions I worked so hard to separate myself from, would become an important part in the process of accepting Alan for who he was.

While my boys were pre-teens, I never talked much about my early years. I continued to want to separate myself from my past and not let those ties strangle my sons. I had had a passion for baseball when I was growing up in Detroit. I made scrapbooks of my favorite teams, clipping newspaper articles daily to capture the accomplishments of the Detroit Tigers. For the first few years of Alan's life, I never took him to a Tigers game and did not watch the games on television. I watched for years as Alan and Andy played soccer at school, never encouraging them to join a baseball team. I rarely talked about my high school days at Detroit Catholic Central, and I certainly did not want them to hear about my troubled college days. I decided to focus upon the present and participate in the school events as they came up.

Alan's quickly deteriorating physical condition in seventh and eighth grade meant he no longer could do most physical activities, such as kicking a ball on the playground. He began to talk about feeling isolated from his classmates. While Andy began to develop physically into a good baseball player, Alan preferred to remain in the van, listening to rock music. I wanted to encourage Andy, but I could not stand by and watch Alan sink into isolation, feeling different and separate because of something beyond his control.

What remained constant as his disease progressed was Alan's looking to me, his dad, for answers and direction. I could not fail him, but I was clueless. I had to get a handle on the situation and take some action to set a vision for him. I became confused over the lack of direction from the doctors. How could they not know what was going on? They had theories but not many facts. What could I possibly provide Alan to give him strength and hope? The one thing I settled on was to share more of myself with Alan, to let him understand me better, and to give him a foundation from which to build. I needed to understand him better as well, to listen to his concerns, fears, and hopes. A bond like that had to bring us all strength, or so I hoped.

I stopped blocking memories and began to recall how I had felt when my own dad entered a room. He looked big and tall. He had ideas and plans for future actions. I drew strength from my dad. I felt a sense of pride just being with him. It had to be the same for Alan; I assumed that he had similar feelings toward me and looked to me for strength, security, and a vision for what could be.

I began to share my past with Alan. I talked about baseball, telling stories about the game. Coincidentally, Tiger Stadium, the home of Detroit Tiger baseball for ninety years, would soon be replaced. I decided to take my sons to games and tell them stories about the old stadium. In response to this, Alan began paying attention to more sports teams. Being very competitive in nature, Alan found great satisfaction in living vicariously through the sports players and their accomplishments.

As a reward for enduring painful tests involving his muscles and nerves, I would buy Alan entire box sets of sports cards. After these sessions, I would sit next to him and carefully open each package of cards slowly, looking at each card and player, talking about the player, and then placing each card carefully into a protective plastic sheet.

I had forgotten how much I had loved baseball. As I began to share with him, I rediscovered myself. The uncertainty over Alan's future seemed to subside as we became more involved in living vicariously through our baseball heroes.

⋄   ⋄   ⋄

Being part of something bigger than oneself, such as baseball, certainly enriches our lives by providing a larger universe of people to associate with. Friendships based upon common ground tend to make people feel closer to each other and more willing to listen and act in a crisis. Alan's first encounter with pneumonia in 2003, while he was in high school, threw us all into a crisis that could have been devastating if not for a belief in something meaningful beyond the disease. People responded in loving ways, performing acts they would never have had the opportunity to do in the normal day-to-day events of life.

⋄   ⋄   ⋄

When Alan was in the hospital that first time with pneumonia, I had never felt so helpless. I had grown up under the influence of a father and mother who solved problems with hard work and smarts. In my case, the hard work and smarts were not working. I could not find a way to help my son. I felt isolated, as I had in my college days.

One evening while driving home from the hospital, fear overwhelmed me. I began crying uncontrollably. In an act

81

of desperation to release my anxiety, I did something I had never imagined possible for me.

I gave up.

I acknowledged the futility of my efforts alone to heal Alan. I released my fear to God and placed it in His hands. I accepted how little control I had over circumstances in my life. A beautiful calm feeling, like a soft blanket warming my bones in the winter, settled over me. Ideas began to pop into my mind. I remembered the name of a teacher who had talked about the power of intuition and faith in bringing about healing. I also recalled articles I had read about doctors recognizing the power of prayer in healing patients.

I called a friend and asked her for help. I wanted her to arrange a special prayer service for Alan. I then called Camille, my former business intuition instructor. I dialed the phone number I had for her, which I was not sure was current. She answered.

I surprised her. After a few minutes of awkward conversation, she finally remembered me. After I explained the situation, she paused for the longest moment. I waited and waited, not sure what to do.

She finally broke the silence and said, "You are the reason I did not leave this morning. I was supposed to leave the country for two weeks but felt a need to wait another day. I have learned from the past never to doubt these feelings. I knew all would be revealed to me if I remained attentive. What do you want from me?"

"Help me save my son's life. I need your guidance."

"Does he want to keep living?" she asked.

"Yes. He had the most beautiful and peaceful smile today. He asked to read the paper for world news. He loves life."

She arranged for a personal friend of hers, a spiritual healer, to visit Alan in the hospital.

After that conversation, I slept for hours, knowing I finally had put something into motion. When I awoke, I saw that I had to hurry to the hospital in time to meet the healer, but then the phone rang. My friend, who had agreed to arrange for a healing prayer session, wanted to provide me with an update that it had been arranged. One family called another, and within several hours the entire community of church friends we had among Alan's school friends had planned a group prayer session for that evening. The pastor had agreed to open the church and several kids offered to say special prayers for Alan. Our friend was so excited and happy to be helping that she almost forgot to tell me another key thing. The Vatican in Rome planned to say a mass at the time of the prayer service. A priest who had known Alan while Alan was in grade school happened to be in Rome and had read the e-mail from the families. He would personally say the mass.

This outpouring of love and the perfect timing of people's response overwhelmed me. The power of love and prayer had been unleashed. I raced back to the hospital. I could not wait to tell Alan and Gwen about what was unfolding.

Alan just looked at me with a calm expression as I explained to him what was happening that evening. He trusted me completely and had that look that said, "I will do whatever you say."

The medical equipment documented the rest. During the day following the visit from the healer and the prayer service, Alan's vital signs improved exponentially. His use of oxygen went from nine liters to two liters. One milestone after another was achieved. Doctors remarked on how quickly he appeared to be gaining strength. Within days, Alan would leave the hospital.

The healing power of prayer and the positive energy of so many people helped raise Alan's spirits, showing him that he was not alone. Many loved him and wanted him to get better. He glowed with excitement after getting home and returning to school. Within twenty-four hours of the prayers, Alan pressured me to get him into his wheelchair so he could go to the computer room down the hall and check his fantasy football teams. Alan had returned to health, and that was all that mattered.

◇ ◇ ◇

How ironic life can be. The family and friends I had tried so hard to maintain a distance from in the past had turned out to be the ones who rallied behind me to help save Alan. My past associations, which I had tried hard to separate from in order to find a new identity, had provided Alan with a foundation, acceptance, spirit, and strength. All of my efforts to keep Alan engaged with others so he would not feel isolated because of his physical disease provided him with the strength to overcome his physical problems and live for his dreams.

◇ ◇ ◇

In subsequent years, I enjoyed similar instances where Alan has found strength in others from their intentions and actions.

A Parent's Thoughts

There exists a necessary duality in life. On the one hand, we need to break free from the expectations of others regarding whom we should be and find our own identity based upon our inner knowledge. But there also exists a powerful unseen force from the prayers and larger intentions of others. Connecting with this force requires us to remain emotionally connected to others so we, too, can join in this larger force of intention.

Insight 7

Find the life force in every moment.

The initial diagnosis of Alan's illness shocked the entire family. Reports from doctors had been inconclusive for several years, giving the family hope that Alan's life would not be shortened. As long as Alan still walked and the nightly exercises kept Alan strong, we lived with hope.

Several people have implied that we lived in denial. I believe our response was more centered on hope and faith that his condition would prove to be less severe than some feared.

My mother personifies the spirit of hope. She is a very beautiful lady with a wonderful heart. Grandma Marcy refers to Alan as "my Alan." She internalizes everything that happens to him as if it were happening to her. Her love for Alan is undeniable, and she would be the first in line to shove Gwen and me aside to offer a transplant or give up her life to save him. Her love and faith, though, leave no room for seeing and accepting Alan's condition. For Marcy, the only reality she expects is to see Alan walking again.

I grew up with this strong faith, and it is deeply embedded within me. I, too, struggled with accepting Alan's illness for fear it could give the illness too much of a foothold. I would rather have stayed fixed upon where I wanted to be and worked toward those outcomes than focus upon the "reality" of the situation and lose hope.

When Alan finally needed the wheelchair full-time, I could no longer avoid the fact that his condition was worsening. My mother, though, reacted the other way. She continued her effort to visualize Alan walking again. She prayed longer for Alan's recovery and told everyone that she believed in her heart that Alan would walk again. She began to more frequently proclaim her vision. Every time she saw Alan, she would say, "I believe you will walk again. I pray for it every night. You will walk again. You do believe this, don't you?"

Alan had grown angry with her saying this to him every time they would see each other. He believed her "attitude of hope" simply denied what was happening. He complained that no one saw him for what he truly was.

I was torn. I believed Alan would get better even as I started researching wheelchair types and prices back when he was in fifth grade. Alan had needed an electric-powered wheelchair, and I would not be able to use my minivan to transport it. I needed a larger van to carry the load of the chair and provide room for the rest of the family. I also needed to move to a new house in 1997 where Alan's room would be on the first floor with Gwen and me so we could be with him day and night. A ramp leading to the door had to be built in the garage, requiring one car to remain outside.

These new needs came at me quickly. Several times I thought it could not be happening that I had to modify my house for my disabled son. I test-drove vans during the week and walked through numerous homes on the weekend, looking for a house to meet our needs. These changes forced me to face Alan's condition head-on. No more pretending things would be okay. The more accommodations I made, the more I felt I was giving up hope for Alan's healing.

These changes, though, brought a new kind of hope in an unexpected way; Alan began to regain independence. He no longer needed to wait for someone to help him walk up a flight of stairs to his bedroom; he just walked down the hall. He began falling less and could enter our new home with minimal assistance. His powerful, motorized wheelchair gave him independence in moving around the house. We all began to feel good again. I looked for more ways to accommodate him. I installed a mini-elevator that could lift Alan and his chair to and from the basement of our home so Alan could experience having friends over to watch movies in the basement family room.

Gwen and I were so full of renewed hope that we opened our hearts to adopt a baby girl from China in 2003. We began the process in 2001. The adoption of Lili brought Alan a new sense of excitement; he had a baby sister to love.

Lili has beautiful eyes, a heart-shaped mouth, and two dimples, one on each side of her nose, that accent her wide smile. Her face glows with life when she laughs. Lili came to us one month after her first birthday. She clung to Gwen for security at first; she let other mothers hold her, but only if she could see that Gwen was not far away. The orphanage where she had lived had many women caregivers, so men were strange creatures to her. My voice, in particular, resonated too deeply for her, and I kept my hands behind my back so she would not feel that I was going to snatch her up. She obviously feared losing Gwen, having fallen in love with this lady who gave her unconditional love, kisses, and hugs. It became obvious that they were two souls matched in heaven.

Lili did find her new brothers fascinating and she accepted Alan at face value. He drove a wheelchair around the house. So what? He needed help eating his food. So did she. They had something in common. In all aspects of life, Lili saw Alan for what he was and she showed full love toward him.

Alan and Lili, 2004. Lili riding on Alan's wheelchair.
Alan is a junior in high school and Lili is two years old.

I began to see Alan through Lili's eyes; no preconceived ideas of what *could be* clouded her vision. This helped me to stop and see what was happening right then in our life. Lili brought smiles from Alan that I had not seen in years. Lili also brought a blessing to us, which eventually saved Alan's life several weeks later.

At lunchtime all throughout Alan's high school years, I traveled to CC to help him with his bathroom needs. Because of Lili, I began to appreciate these brief, ten-minute events. I stopped feeling frustrated over having to see my son in this physical condition and began to appreciate the moment. I looked forward to seeing him, asking him how his day was going, and straightening his shirt if necessary. The moments I most enjoyed were when Alan would tell me about a debate he had had with a teacher or classmate on topics like welfare, discrimination, politics, or sports. Alan, forever the champion of the underdog, reveled in matching wits with deserving foes. His arms moved with a bit more strength when he explained in splendid detail the finer points of the discussion. I said nothing during those moments; I was just happy to be listening to his ideas and feeling the energy of his youth.

Delving into the eternal, existential questions of mankind, like good vs. evil, happiness vs. despair, being vs. nothingness, kept Alan thinking beyond his physical condition. On days when he became excited over a new idea or discovery, the ever-present pain in his body magically disappeared, if ever so briefly.

What I came to realize was that Alan mentally projected himself beyond the pain and frustration of his everyday existence. He projected toward things beyond what we typically think of in our day-to-day lives. When Lili arrived, Alan had another thing to focus upon. We could not provide him enough detail regarding Lili's day and what she had done. He insisted upon kissing her before bed, wanted pictures of Lili in his room, and proudly bragged about his little sister to the guys at CC.

The first Friday of his three-week stay at the University of Michigan Hospital in 2003, we brought Lili with us to sit with Alan. Lili had just begun to speak English. One of her first words was "Alan." While we all sat around Alan's bed, Lili began to shout, with great excitement, our names. She began saying "Mommy, Andy, Daddy, Alan" loudly and with great sweetness in her voice. Just as Alan would excitedly tell me about his recent debates and new ideas while I helped him at lunch, Alan's face lit up when Lili spoke his name, his cheeks glowing red, his blue eyes piercing, and his arms moving. Not since he had entered the hospital had Alan looked so strong.

Again, viewing Alan as Lili did, with complete acceptance for who he was in the moment, helped me to accept the fact that he was getting worse physically. This simple acknowledgment brought with it a deep feeling of calm. Then I remembered the words of the spiritual healer Mary Carey when she visited Alan in the hospital. "You must relax and place the burden in God's hands so you can then be calm and receptive to the healing graces. You need to realize," she said, "that only when you unconditionally accept those around you, will you open yourself and your family to the eternal flow of blessings from God." She mentioned that Lili, like all children, is capable of bringing this healing force with her because of her unconditional acceptance and love of others. Lili brought healing to Alan.

My body tingled all over when I heard those words. A very deep sense of calm, unlike any I had ever felt, came over me. I breathed slower, my mouth muscles relaxed, and I sighed, acknowledging a truth as I had never realized it before. I had to look at my situation as Lili did. I had to become childlike in my unconditional love of others before I could help heal Alan. I saw the impact Lili had upon Alan. I felt like a truth about life had been given to me.

Since this realization, I have worked hard to be more open and less judgmental. I now understand that there will be times when I need to let the energy, creativity, and people come to me rather than always being proactive, trying to force the issues and actions to conform to my needs and desires. Understanding when to just let things flow meant I had to learn to see the circumstances as they truly were, watching with less personal interpretation in order to find out what energy and ideas were being revealed. My own patience with others, listening instead of talking, became my critical tool of survival.

When Alan returned home from the 2003 hospital stay, he had many issues that needed to be resolved. He had missed a very important test, the PSAT. A high PSAT score translates into qualification for the National Merit Scholarship and recognition for academic achievements. Alan had set the PSAT as a key milestone to establish his place in society as a very bright young man who could achieve great things in spite of his physical problems.

No makeups are allowed for the PSAT. A miss is a miss. When I first heard this, I immediately wanted to know whom I should talk to so Alan could get an exemption from this silly rule. After all, Alan had just recovered from pneumonia. However, I did not immediately have time to take care of this; many doctor appointments had to be addressed. I decided to let this PSAT issue be my first test in letting people and opportunities come to me rather than trying to make something happen.

The school counselor understood the importance of the PSAT to Alan. Although it proved to be difficult, I just let her pursue the options, deciding I would let it all flow to me—the ideas, the people, the opportunities, and so on.

Remarkably for me, a guy who grew up believing I had to make all things happen or nothing would occur, events began to unfold right before my eyes. A director of the PSAT arranged for Alan to take the SAT in January. The SAT would be graded in a way to adjust for differences between the PSAT and the SAT. Alan would have to take a second SAT to test writing skills in order to complete the PSAT requirements. The timing for these tests worked perfectly for Alan's recovery time. January and May would be the timing, with results fed into the PSAT program. The site at which Alan was to take the SAT was scheduled to be in an unsafe neighborhood in a building that had not been updated to accommodate a wheelchair. Again, I just let the people around us do their thing. Within one week, CC had received permission to administer the test onsite. Several teachers readily volunteered to come in on their day off to conduct the test.

All the counselors, administrators of the PSAT/SAT, and teachers at CC appeared to jump at the chance to make a difference for Alan. I did not worry about any of these issues. A very warm feeling within me confirmed that all would work out well.

And it did. Alan took the SAT in January, scoring in the top one percent of the nation. He became a National Merit Semi-Finalist for his top scores. With those results, Alan could apply to the schools of his dreams, knowing he had a critical piece of the equation in place.

This "uncontrollable" flow of people and events appearing in our lives at just the right moment did not end with the PSAT episode. One final high school event, the yearly Academic Awards Banquet, confirmed this beneficial flow of life for the good of Alan.

I arrived a few minutes late one Monday in May at Alan's school to help him with his lunchtime needs. On my way over to the school that day, I had started to reminisce about the many times over the past four years when I had come during my lunch hour. As I walked in, I noticed that Alan's face looked a bit disappointed as he sat in the doorway. I alerted myself for almost anything, but I entered the school with a smile.

"How are things going, Al?" A more direct question like "Why do you look so sad?" would only have forced him to deny feeling sad.

Just small talk occurred between us at first. I did not want to risk probing his sadness. I was just about ready to leave the building when Alan said, "Dad." He said it in such a way that I knew he wanted to talk.

"Do you need some cash?" I asked.

"Yeah, a few bucks would be good," he replied.

As I placed the money in his bag on the back of his chair, he said, "You know, the Academic Awards Banquet? I am not sure I want to go."

I could not believe I was hearing this from him. For four years I had heard nothing but what a great event this was— the Emmys of academic achievement. We had attended for three years. Only seniors receive the big awards, like scholarships. For three years, Alan had dreamed of receiving a scholarship and recognition for what he had achieved.

"Oh, come on," I said. "You have to go. Why would you want to miss?"

I noticed his eyes looked watery. He knew something. I tried hard to remain calm and crafty, but I began to feel rage growing inside over what I began to speculate was a slight to Alan. I had always harbored a fear that in the end awards for seniors would go to the bright, physically fit guys, those who appeared to have the most certain future. I had hoped this would not happen, but I knew people and money could create ugly outcomes at times.

"Dad, I looked at the listing of names for the banquet and I did not find a code by my name, indicating I will not receive one of the special senior awards."

"Are you sure?" I spat out, trying to not give in to my worst anger.

"Go look for yourself."

Sure enough, no code.

"Who did get the codes?" I asked.

"The usual names," Alan said.

"But you are among the usual. What happened?"

"I do not know," Alan said, rather abruptly. "I have to go back to class."

Alan and I had worked so hard filling out applications that winter. He had around a 4.5 grade-point average, among the best in the school. I did not understand.

When I came home that night from work, I went straight to Alan and said, "We are still going to the awards banquet."

He nodded yes. He looked happier now. "Did you find out something else beyond what we talked about today?"

"No, but I do want to go, if for no other reason than to make them feel uneasy."

I met Gwen, Alan, and Andy at the banquet on Thursday of that week. As soon as I entered the hall, I could hear Alan calling me.

"Dad, Dad! Look at the program. I now have a special code next to my name."

"Do you know what it is for?

"No idea."

Thank you, God, I thought. I truly did not care exactly what he would receive. I just did not want him to feel snubbed.

The banquet hall was full. I had heard for years about how smart Alan's class was, the brightest to come through the school in years. Many of the guys would be receiving special recognition. Many families had grandparents with them. We did, too. My mother came with me to the hall.

Large crystal chandeliers hung from the twenty-two-foot ceilings, creating beautiful designs of shapes and color on the walls. All the guys wore suits and ties, reminding me of the movies about prep schools, like *Dead Poets Society*.

At our table sat a youthful-looking mom with her son, a sophomore at the school. She beamed with pride. She sat next to me, so I heard all the stories of her son's accomplishments and how she, indeed, was an actress—a quite accomplished actress, at that. She did not probe into who my son was. Finally, she pointed toward Andy and asked, "Is that your son?"

I said, "Yes."

"And what will he be receiving today?"

"He will not receive an award today." I did not offer anything more, for I knew what she was thinking.

She looked a bit puzzled but also convinced that she had the upper hand in terms of whose son was most accomplished. She finally could not take it anymore and had to ask, "Are you here for a friend?"

Alan sat right next to me. For some reason, she had not assumed Alan was a student who would be receiving an award.

"My son, Alan, over here, will be receiving an award today."

"Oh," she said and looked away.

My guess is that she did not believe Alan could achieve such things, looking so frail and uncomfortable in his chair. But I just let this pass. As always, I kept to the business of taking care of what I had responsibility for. Let others think what they might. I sat and listened to her self-absorbed monologue.

Every year at the event we would sit on the far side of the room. The aisles were wider and easier for Alan to maneuver around with the chair. At dinner time, people were allowed to walk to the buffet line, several at a time, starting with the center of the room. We, therefore, were last to get food.

Since we were one of the last to eat, the award ceremonies always started while we were still eating. Fortunately, since our last name begins with "O," we had time before Alan would receive anything since the awards were given in alphabetical order.

The presentation of special awards for seniors takes place at the end of the event, meaning Alan could go to the stage twice, once for his yearly accomplishments and once for the special recognition award. We had no idea what he would receive. Alan and I began making small wagers on what he would get. I thought he would receive one of the less-grand awards, thinking that he would be a runner-up for the more significant awards.

I lost a few dollars to Alan that night. Fifteen special awards were given in total to the students. After losing ten bucks at Alan, I finally looked at him and said, "Do you think you will be getting one of the top five?"

Alan never looked nervous. He only slightly acknowledged my comment. We just sat silently listening to the next awards. One by one, other names were called. Five awards remained.

Alan's good friend, Charlie, had not yet been called. Both Alan and I were certain that of the two remaining, Alan would get the next one, with the top award going to Charlie. Charlie had the highest GPA ever achieved in the school's history and was valedictorian of his graduating class. He was also the nicest, most honest guy you could ever meet.

Alan already had his hand ready on his chair control to go to receive the next award. He had even started moving through the aisles when the next name called was Charlie's.

Alan had already gone up a few yards from the table so I could not just lean over and talk to him. What I will never forget is when our eyes met. Neither one of us could believe it. He would win the top academic award of the night. He nodded at me and I nodded back. Memories of the past four years rushed through my mind.

It might be nice if I took a picture of the moment, I thought to myself. I started walking to the front of the room.

I saw the school principal and staff assembling on the stage. Looking back, I think they all wanted to be there when Alan received the award.

The last award was named after a former Catholic Central graduate who had lived with a great spirit for life. Nothing had been impossible to him. He had graduated with honors, having overcome a childhood of problems from living in a neighborhood in Detroit. He had died in a tragic accident. The law firm he had worked for in Chicago created a scholarship award of $5,000, to be given to a CC grad who exhibited the traits of this deceased grad.

On that night, the president of the law firm had flown to Detroit from Chicago to present the award personally. In his speech, he emphasized how the current recipient exemplified a spirit for life unlike any other over the years. When reviewing the written applications, he and his staff believed that one applicant stood out as the most unique and poignant for demonstrating how a person could overcome any situation. It was the spirit of life that the law firm wanted to recognize and reward. Typically most recipients had been chosen after a long discussion, but not this year. This year, the choice had been simple and amazing. He then announced, with great pleasure, that the recipient was Alan Omilian.

Tears flowed from my eyes. I hurried to the front of the room to catch the moment. My camera bounced on my hip as I hurried into camera-ready position. The capacity crowd rose to its feet—which I had never seen occur in the previous years I had attended the event. I snapped several shots of Alan receiving the standing ovation.

Not quite sure what to do, Alan shook his head in acknowledgment and rode back to the table. The event was over, but families hung around. Dads from the other side of the large room, some who had known Alan since first grade, stood in a makeshift line to personally congratulate him. The actress-mom at our table kept saying, "I had no idea my table would have the highest award recipient at it." She looked stunned—her assumptions regarding Alan did not match reality.

The lead partner of the law firm that had awarded Alan the $5,000 scholarship sat with Alan for thirty-five minutes, discussing Alan's plans. He also talked about his own life, what he had planned for, and how some things had just never happened. He looked so comfortable talking with Alan, revealing some things about himself to someone whom he felt would understand and respect him.

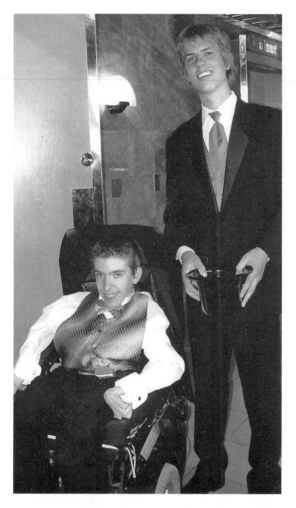

Alan and friend Mitch, high school graduation celebration.

Days later, after we all had enjoyed that truly joyous event, I reflected on what had occurred. Mary Carey's words kept coming back to me—relax and let the flow of life come to me. Find a way to belong to the flow. All the time I had been dealing with Alan's illness, I had been working on following these words. Rather than trying to assert my will upon events, I practiced looking for the flow, the insights from God to guide my actions. I found that several dads had hired attorneys to write their kids' applications for scholarships and entrance applications to colleges. I did not do that. Instead, I reminded myself to identify the talent within Alan to write well and let that speak for itself.

To this day, the concept of understanding the moment has never failed me. The less I try to control the moment, the more assistance I receive. Additionally, the more I believe in this, the more frequently special people and events come into our lives to bless us with their kind actions.

A Parent's Thoughts

Even though I have provided some great examples of believing in the moment and not trying to force issues, I find it difficult to consistently do this. I have found daily meditation trains my mind to stop, listen, and observe before reacting.

Deciding to Believe

2007

I kept hearing the words "Just keep working with me, Al" as I drove home. Where had this young male nurse been until today? In the three weeks that Alan had been in the hospital, I had never seen him on Alan's floor. His words of hope and of having a plan contrasted in my heart with the words of the doctors, who had given Alan less than a ten percent chance of continuing to live without the use of a permanent ventilator. Although the tracheotomy would be a quick procedure, Alan's ability to speak again would be in doubt. The tracheotomy would change the airflow around the vocal chords and Alan would have to adapt. He would be able to speak, I was sure, but his voice would not likely sound the same, which would impact his voice-recognition equipment.

Speaking is everything for Alan. The tube that had been down his throat for the past three weeks to pull mucus from his lungs had nearly destroyed his will to live. Would the tracheotomy have the same negative impact? In reality, we probably did not have a choice, I thought as I pulled into the parking lot of my favorite eatery. It was lunchtime and I needed some comfort food.

Nothing reminds me of happier times as much as a Coney Island. We often stopped at such a place for quick food when we were traveling the country on our family road trips.

Andy's travel baseball team would go to this type of restaurant when they were playing games in various parts of the country. I can still see Alan walking with me into these places, holding my hand for support.

A hot turkey sandwich with gravy and mashed potatoes was the perfect choice. Rather than go home after lunch and be alone with my thoughts, I decided to go to work. There I could find a few hours of relief from what would certainly be a difficult forty-eight hours. "Just keep working with me, Al" resonated more in my heart. Those words gave me hope that hard work could deliver results. I understood that— work hard to obtain better things. But what would be the better things?

Gwen called me on my cell just as I left work for the night. She told me about the workout Alan had gotten from the nurse. He had tired Alan so much that Alan was sleeping more soundly than he had in over a month. She decided to stay the night; I could have the night off. That meant sleeping in my own bed.

The next morning, I left early to go to work. I wanted to be at the hospital before lunch so I could speak with the team of doctors. An early start would free up time during lunch. I repeatedly checked my watch all morning just to be certain I left in time. Several last-minute problems came up just as I planned to leave; my anxiety level jumped sky high along with my blood pressure. I did not want to miss my opportunity to talk with the doctors.

Just then my cell phone rang.

"Hello?"

"Mr. Omilian?"

"Yes."

"This is Alan's doctor at the University of Michigan."

"What's wrong?"

"Nothing's wrong. I just want to be sure you plan to be at the hospital at noon today. We need to talk with you and your wife."

"I am trying to leave now. I'm having some problems here, but I will get there as soon as I can."

"Mr. Omilian. Do your best. I do not want to get into much detail over the phone, but I need to tell you that I did not expect to see this from Alan."

I got the proverbial lump in my throat. What had happened?

"Yesterday I told you that Alan had a ten percent chance of recovery without the need of a ventilator. I do not know what happened overnight, but I am ready to let him go home today without a ventilator. His lungs are completely clear."

"What did you just say?"

"I know, I know. I am just as surprised. Just come soon."

When I arrived, the room was filled with people. Alan sat in his bed, upright and bright-eyed. Those blue eyes beamed with life and energy. One nurse was packing a bag. Another was washing Alan's face and hair. The pulmonary specialist, a wonderful man who never once acted annoyed by Alan's constant requests for bed adjustments, stood next to Alan. He looked focused.

I tried to work my way into the room and wave. No luck. Where was Gwen? For three weeks I had sat with Alan in this room, watching the start of summer unfold outside the small window. I could see the tennis players in the distance running up and down the twelve courts below. Bicyclists rode through the nature trails just to the left of the courts. I watched them day and night as I sat with Alan alone in this room. I never knew if the day would come when Alan would leave.

I stood by myself on the outside looking in on the action. Everyone seemed energized. They all loved Alan and wanted to check off a success for their efforts. Several nights earlier, two young men had died on that same floor, one from a heart attack and another from pneumonia. This time they could claim a victory.

A voice coming from my side said, "He is looking good, isn't he, Dad?"

I must have looked startled.

"It's okay, Dad. Alan and I worked hard yesterday. We did my plan."

I wanted to talk to him more, but just then the pulmonary specialist was ready to pull the tube out of Alan's throat. As I stepped forward to watch, I heard the male nurse say, "I need to be going. I have another patient to take care of."

And just like that, the man with the plan exited our lives as quickly as he had entered twenty-four hours earlier.

As the tube came out, Alan's eyes met mine. We smiled. He talked. Oh, did he talk. Gwen had entered the room just as the tube came out. Alan began giving commands to all regarding what he needed. He was back.

To this day, I still think about the young man who had appeared out of nowhere and stared right at me, declaring his plan to bring Alan back. Like the priest from Africa, he understood what needed to be done and he did it. The actions of both of those men showed me that we are never truly alone in our time of fear. We need to look for the special people who appear at the right moment to help.

Insight 8

We cannot predict the journey of our lives; live in awe, wonderment, and thankfulness.

Alan left the hospital following his second experience with pneumonia in 2007, determined to fulfill his dreams. Unfortunately, new barriers emerged to challenge his determination. The emotional trauma caused by the inability to speak turned into a psychological problem rather quickly. For several weeks, Alan could not tolerate being alone in his room. Although physically cleared of pneumonia, Alan still felt terror in his heart. The thought "What if no one can hear me?" tortured his soul, even though one of us was always within one room of him. Out of sight truly seemed "out of mind" to Alan; he feared being left alone.

Panic became a partner with his physical disability in the daily assault upon Alan's determination to live a life filled with the same hopes and dreams as his buddies.

We traveled to Pennsylvania that summer for a reunion of the families who had adopted children from China. The gathering was to be in Lancaster. I reserved the largest hotel room possible, knowing that Alan and Andy would most likely spend much time in the room. Andy was all set. He brought his X-Box game system, along with his baseball, football, basketball, and hockey game discs. In his mind, this would be a week of video game fun. Alan loved the Internet and all of its possibilities. He had planned to spend his hours working on it. This trip distracted Alan from his fears. For that week and then a week at a lakeside cottage in northern Michigan, Alan experienced no mental terrors. He looked relaxed and ready to go.

Alan with family in 2006, visiting Grandpa up north in Indian River, Michigan. Alan's first year of college.

When Alan graduated from high school, he had been accepted at Notre Dame University and the University of Michigan. We visited Notre Dame first since this was the place Alan always dreamed of attending. The ride to the school was five hours so we decided to stay the night. The academic dean walked us around campus, and Alan saw the dorm room they would provide, actually two rooms to accommodate Alan and his live-in aide. The school could not assist in funding the aide, so the total cost of attending would be nearly $50,000 per year. That night, over dinner, Alan and I both knew this would not work. The University of Michigan would have to be the choice.

U of M offered Alan a full-ride scholarship and a place in their special Residential College, an independent unit of U of M that required high academic achievement and an interest in a wide variety of subjects. The Residential College, it turned out, offered Alan a fantastic opportunity to develop his writing skills. The full-ride scholarship, based upon his academic achievements in high school, made him feel very special and proud. Alan's first two years at U of M were magical. In addition to no physical setbacks, he discovered many new books to read and loved taking classes with professors who had traveled the world and had written the books they read in class.

The 2007 fall semester, following his second hospital stay, became his best in academic achievement. He felt involved again in the day-to-day activities of life. His breathing was strong. Physically, he maneuvered his chair better than ever before. He also kept the terror attacks under control.

I clearly remember the night when things began to unravel. Alan assumed he would have a two-week break between semesters. Because he had worked until the very last day of the 2007 fall semester finishing a term paper with an all-night effort, Alan especially looked forward to a nice rest period during the Christmas holidays.

On the evening after Christmas Day, while at the Motor City Bowl college football game at Ford Field in Detroit, one of Alan's friends said that he would not have to return to school until January 15. Then he said, "Too bad you go back January 2."

I saw the look on Alan's face. He had not realized the return to school would be so early. All the way home, he talked continuously about having only a few days left to relax.

On January 1, a major snowstorm hit the Ann Arbor and Detroit area. Snow removal at U of M was very slow due to the large amount of snow. Alan had to ride through large clumps of freshly plowed snow just to get to class. The winds were strong and cold. Alan felt exhausted after the first day, and that evening he felt sick to his stomach. He had come down with a touch of the flu. He wasn't sick enough to stay home, but he was tired enough that his every effort felt twice as difficult.

Finally, Alan's exhaustion from the previous semester combined with the difficult start of the winter semester wore him down. He stayed home the entire week to sleep and fell behind in his classwork. His hand could no longer stay on the control toggle of his wheelchair for long periods of time; his arm would slip off the control, causing him to call for help frequently.

This made every trip to campus more and more frustrating. One day, Alan became so frustrated that he just stopped in transit to a class and began to curse. His aide, Beverly, called me at work. She sounded very concerned.

"Can you come to Ann Arbor? We are in the Anthropology Biology building."

Long pause.

"Alan cannot move."

Beverly had never called, so I knew it had to be serious. I left a meeting at work and rushed to Ann Arbor, a twenty-minute ride at best. When I found Alan and Beverly in the hallway, Alan looked dejected. I rubbed his arm gently and asked him what was wrong. At first, he complained about his arm. I turned on his chair and placed his hand on the toggle. His arm looked fine, but the chair did not move. I checked the emergency brake lever. No problem there. I checked the wires. No apparent problem there, either. However, the chair appeared to be broken.

I finally coaxed it to work, tapping on a wire while I turned the machine on and off.

This chair had been Alan's mechanical legs since he had been in seventh grade. The foam in the seat had molded over time to support every movement Alan made. Stickers of racing cars, rock bands, and his high school logo hung proudly on the back. Scuff marks and chipped paint remained as a testimony to Alan's mighty goalie saves while playing wheelchair hockey.

The balding tires on the chair, along with the faltering mechanisms, necessitated a change. Our wheelchair distributor had already advised me to order a new chair. We did order a newer version of the chair, hoping to minimize any transition issues from old to new. This newer chair had just been delivered when the older one broke.

Alan panicked over the idea of changing chairs; his old black, front-wheel-drive "Permobile" chair responded to the slightest touch of the control knob. The chair moved freely through the toughest corners, never impeding Alan's ability to move in any direction, avoiding oncoming walkers. The new chair did not have the same touch and feel. Since the insurance company would not consider repairing the older chair, Alan had no choice but to try the new one. Progress was slow and Alan continued to ask for help to move his chair as he finished the winter semester.

The transition to the new chair and Alan's continued physical decline created tremendous anxiety. Fortunately, we had our yearly one-week summer vacation to northern Michigan as a time to calm down and regroup.

One evening during our stay in northern Michigan, we were leaving a wonderful roadside restaurant. We had just eaten a dinner of fresh Michigan walleye. The evening sun was setting over the lake across the street. We strolled by one-hundred-year-old pines, windswept at angles to accommodate the harsh winter winds. As we walked through the parking lot of the Northside Inn, everyone felt relaxed and satisfied. We breathed in the cool, fresh air pouring down from the elder pines.

There were only a few customers at the restaurant that evening. With the parking lot relatively free of cars, I looked at Alan and said, "Let's try riding your chair here in the lot."

I must have caught Alan in a moment of peace—he readily agreed. For ten minutes, he made maneuvers with this new chair almost as well as he had with the old chair. He smiled with great confidence. Hope once again took over his big blue eyes. I stopped him short of getting tired; it had been months since he had last tried. Alan's sense of hope grew over the summer.

"Maybe this new chair can work after all," he confided in me several times.

Alan's 2008 fall semester approached quickly once we returned from vacation. With eighteen credit hours left until his graduation from U of M, Alan's fall semester would be pivotal to achieving his plans to graduate in the spring of 2009. I took the day off from work on Alan's first day back so that I could help him find the classrooms and identify the best routes to and from his classes.

The day was hot and humid—85°F at eight o'clock in the morning was not a good omen. Parking would be tight since everyone was returning from summer break. Alan had three classes in a row with ten-minute breaks in between. The classes were in three different buildings.

I had prepared myself. With several hundred dollars of cash in my pocket, two credit cards, Alan's student ID, and a copy of his course schedule including course numbers, instructor's names, and sequence numbers, I set off to get this semester started in a positive way.

Alan looked nervous. Doubt crept into his mind. "What if my hand falls off the chair toggle? What if the doors are too narrow? What if the classroom doors do not easily accommodate the new chair? What if I get tired? What if my breathing becomes shallow? What if I look like a spectacle to the other students?" Alan shared these thoughts with me as we drove to Ann Arbor.

Getting out of the van, Alan confided, "I do not want to look like I am making my last bold trek up the mountain before I die. I do not want to look pitiful."

His first class had a basement entrance with a long, curving hallway leading to the classroom. Alan could not hold his hand on the toggle that morning, so his aide, Beverly, and I controlled the chair from the side. It was not his preferred approach, but we got him into the room. I could only hope for better as the day progressed.

I had forty-five minutes to buy books from two bookstores and walk to the next building on the mission of finding the right entrance in advance. The day became hotter as I walked the busy Ann Arbor streets. Kids talked about movies, concerts, and parties as I passed. I sometimes cringed with pain, knowing my son could not do any of those things. For Alan, just making it from class to class in his new chair would be success.

I felt exhausted by the end of the day. Alan did not say much, but he must have felt the same. Would my efforts on this opening day pay off? Could Alan get a good start to the semester?

The answer quickly became "no." The next few days were a disaster. One class was moved to another building, a place that was more difficult to enter. Alan could no longer use his arm to move the toggle, and maneuvering his chair through the buildings became more difficult for Beverly. She tried her best to guide the chair while walking at its side and moving the toggle handle forward and sideways, but slamming into doorways and the continuous starting and stopping of the chair for redirection became too frustrating.

After a few days of this, Alan decided to stop attending classes. Beverly offered to go to his classes and record the lectures. In itself, this could have worked. However, Alan began to feel more and more isolated and depressed. He could no longer control his own chair. He could no longer attend classes. Sitting up straight in the chair had become painful—a rib had begun to protrude from his left side due to the increased curvature in his back and the bone rubbed against his hip when he sat up in the chair. The lower left bone of his ribcage was also pressing upon the skin. This area began rubbing against his leg when he sat up straight in his chair. We placed sterile patches over the wound to prevent further bleeding and irritation. The doctor's only remedy was to keep Alan sitting further back in his chair.

This wound took weeks to heal. One evening in early November, in the silence of midnight, Alan decided he had had enough. No more school. No more going out. No more hope. The panic attacks returned. His high-pitched screams for help became a nightly event. I jumped the first time I heard them. Dark thoughts entered my mind, and I thought he was having a heart attack or his lungs had collapsed. We ran into his room, expecting the worst. Instead we found Alan asleep. We woke him and asked what was wrong. He had no idea what we were talking about. He was having nightmares but did not realize it until we woke him up.

In the daytime, he was exhausted from his restless sleep. The panic attacks continued for weeks. During the day, he grew more and more anxious, once again acting panic-stricken if we left his sight. We called the medical agency for help.

Maintaining a vision for the future and looking beyond present difficulties no longer felt like options. Life began to cave in on Alan, with little hope for the future. A combination of having to become accustomed to a new chair, suffering with an open ribcage wound, adjusting to a weakening arm, failing to finish his college classes, and fending off the growing feeling of loneliness all had become too much. Isolation, depression, and anxiety filled the void.

A young woman named Sylvia, a psychologist, began to visit Alan three times a week. She was nearly six feet tall and big-boned, but slender. Her delicate mannerisms emphasized her very cautious and deliberate speech. I characterized her as very respectful in her actions and words, careful not to establish an opinion too quickly.

Sylvia would never be the first person to talk in a room full of people. She observed, taking note of sounds, physical objects, and the facial expressions of others. Her non-judgmental nature immediately created a sense of ease in those around her.

During the first week of therapy with Sylvia, Alan was angrier than usual. He demanded everything from drugs to food, displaying zero tolerance for delays. I wondered what good the sessions were if all we received was more anger from Alan.

Week two showed a little improvement. Alan began to talk cryptically about what was going on in his head. Several times he said, "I might as well just stay at home and watch my sports games and movies and enjoy the time I have left."

Those words made my heart sink. He appeared to be giving up, resigning himself to living out what he believed was left of his life. One night, he finally confided in me.

"I have lost the ability to do all I had learned to enjoy. I can no longer go to school, drive my chair, or sit up straight. I will not try anymore. I do not have the strength. I am not what I used to be."

"Nor am I," I said rather quickly. "I just turned fifty and when I see myself in the mirror, I think I look old. This happened almost overnight. I am no longer part of the younger crowd, and people call me 'sir.' I have become the guy who appears to have been at the company forever."

Alan's remarks triggered something in me. I truly understood him. Alan recognized he could no longer be the person he once was, no matter what he tried. I couldn't either; my possibilities suddenly were different from what they had appeared to be just moments before.

The best we have is the here and now. Living in the moment suddenly became more than a concept, but rather a reality. Alan stated the true reality of life that evening in that we only have the now. We cannot go back. Alan was facing up to his present condition and he was dragging me along. Sylvia was helping him accept this.

One evening, Alan and I were watching football. Out of nowhere, Alan asked if I knew how he could take the rest of his classes online in order to graduate from the University of Michigan. It was the first time in many weeks that he had shown an interest in school. It was mid-December, so I had one, maybe two weeks to figure out a plan before winter term registration would be full. Online classes for the advanced courses Alan required did not exist; instructors wanted in-class participation.

A television commercial gave me an idea. A webcam used by families to share the Christmas moment could also be used to share the classroom experience. I checked with the university regarding my webcam idea. They appeared surprised at first, as if I were the first to ask about this. In what appeared to be a flat-footed response, they said they needed to know more about my approach in order to become comfortable with the idea. With this tentative agreement in hand, I purchased the webcam and set it up on Beverly's computer.

I remember watching the first landing of men on the moon. I sat with my mother and brother and cheered with pride as my mother cried with delight. I ran outside several times to look at the moon, hoping to see the U.S. flag on it.

You would have thought we were celebrating a similar event when, on a snowy morning in January, Beverly and Alan did the first webcam hook-up from the classroom. Gwen and I huddled over Alan's laptop. The time was one minute after nine o'clock.

"Where is she?" Gwen asked.

"Don't worry, she'll be there. I went over the exact steps with her last night and even wrote them down."

The computer began to buzz. This was it! The call was coming in from Beverly. Alan, cool-headed as ever, answered.

"Hello. Hi. Okay."

No famous memorable words.

Suddenly, the laptop screen filled with the face of a professor beginning his lecture. Just like that, Alan had a way to finish his coursework.

Those big blue eyes were sharp again. The anticipation in Alan's face told me we had adapted to the changed circumstances. Technology once again gave Alan a chance to participate and ensured his right to a meaningful life.

I could not be certain how long this new approach would last. I thought of numerous possibilities for using the webcam to keep Alan engaged in life, free from feelings of isolation and fear.

More important than the technology was our unrelenting desire to keep Alan involved in life. He had a right to life like all of us. It did take extra effort to make this happen, but his struggles forced me to test the limits of my resourcefulness and determination. I felt more alive and aware because of this continuous challenge. This was, in the end, my reward—feeling more alive and seeing more life in Alan and in his beautiful big blue eyes.

In a remarkably unpredictable way, the journey for Alan continues. In many ways, the limits of his life's journey are defined by any limits Gwen and I place upon ourselves in helping him live the life God has chosen for him. Alan's struggles remind me daily of how fragile our existence is. In my folly, I may believe I have control over my destiny. In reality, however, I must be comfortable with change. Alan's case stands out because of his physical limitations, but all of my children require the same vigilance and ready-to-react approach that I give Alan.

A Parent's Thoughts

Spend one day emphasizing the moment. Make no plans for the day. Just observe yourself and everyone around you. Hear the issues of those around you. Look into their eyes. Do not judge them in your mind. Keep quiet and listen. Be aware for life-changing moments.

Insight 9

Embrace your personal journey.

What happens when two mighty forces coexist? What happens when a "never give up" attitude confronts an unrelenting disease? The story of my son Alan reveals how seemingly contradictory forces must coexist if life is to have meaning and purpose. The struggle raises awareness and motivates action. With Alan, maintaining a constant vision of possibilities for the future projected him toward achievements that could not have been anticipated or planned. He has remained positive, living with curiosity and anticipation, even when the physical reality continued to grow grim.

As the years moved on, the need to live in the moment became apparent. For Alan, his best physical moment was right now. So how could he make plans and be fully involved in his future, yet live in the moment? One way was to embrace his life as a journey, like the family road trips, measured by the intensity of experiences and less by the length of time.

A journey typically exposes the traveler to new and unexpected moments. He relies upon all of his senses and emotions to navigate the unexpected and unfamiliar. When Alan accepted his journey, he began to appreciate the details of life with greater feeling and intensity.

One evening in late October 2009, I heard the phone ring on Alan's computer. The time was midnight. For several weeks, Alan had been feeling depressed, frustrated over not being more involved in the daily affairs of life. He wanted to find a job as a writer. His body, however, drained him of his life's energy. I had been trying to find ways to help Alan sleep better at night.

"Hi, sure, I have some time. Okay. Just read me what you have."

This conversation continued for nearly two hours. I could not hear the other end of the discussion and wondered who this was he was talking with. I finally fell asleep. In the morning, Alan was sleeping, better than I had seen in weeks. When I returned home from work that evening, he was on the phone again, completely engaged in some project. Alan simultaneously researched the web, saved files, called people for information, and looked full of life. A rosy color had returned to his cheeks. He ate well. When finished for that evening, he fell asleep before I could talk with him and find out what was going on. I felt left out but enjoyed seeing him fully absorbed in the moment, working on something of significance to him and to others.

During the ensuing three days, Alan found a shelter from the thoughts of the past and the fears of the future. He found peace and fulfillment in this moment of time when he had laser-like vision about his project. He was sharing his talents and making connections with ideas and friends. Alan chose to believe again in the goodness and power of life as he found a way to contribute in spite of his failing body.

◊   ◊   ◊

As this one special experience demonstrates, living in the moment begins with a focus upon something tangible and positive, including a chance to participate with others to achieve a goal. A stronger sense of purpose and connection to others often results.

◊　◊　◊

The eight concepts discussed in the previous chapters heighten our observations and help us become more grounded in the present. I have begun to realize that my response to events is more important in defining who I am than the things that are happening to me. How do I maintain hope in the present moment? It can be as simple as saying, "I feel good" to myself as the first step toward making the positive emerge. A kind word to another person can spark hope in that person by making him or her feel like everything is not so bad. In the present moment, I can look for the "choices of the heart" that are available to me, those choices that I feel are inherently right for me. For example, I often felt right to just sit with Alan and listen to his thoughts, even though I could choose to complete one of the items on my "to-do" list instead. Often this heartfelt choice proved to be perfect for that moment, giving Alan companionship when he most needed it. The "to-do" list will always be there.

In the moment, I can become aware of the people around me. The awareness of the moment forces me to focus on who is there and what they are saying and keeps me from thinking about something coming up in the future or trying to figure out what the next thing is that I want to say. I can be a friendlier man to others if I am giving full attention to what others are saying or doing. Remaining quiet and calm helps me remain in the present moment and prevents me from allowing my thoughts to wander to the past or future.

The miracles of life occur in the present. With the clouds of the past and the anxiety over the future lifted, I can clearly see the amazing people and life-changing events occurring before my eyes. Where were these miracles before? They were always there but were blurry to me because of my preoccupation with things beyond my control.

Taking the time to look around, right now, and see, hear, touch, and smell makes it impossible to feel isolated. How can I be isolated when I have so much to observe? Life becomes fun again, as it was when I was a child—when the kaleidoscope of life becomes real.

Connections among people and events become clear when we take the time to look. What appears to be "coincidences" begin to happen more often. The right person with the perfect idea appears when needed. These events and the positive energy they bring lift my spirits, helping me to feel hopeful and happy. The less I try to control people and events, trying to get people to do things *my way*, the more receptive I become to these encounters. In a seemingly contradictory way, the less I try to control events and people, the more things occur that bring me closer to what I want to achieve.

So, living life as a journey, as I have with Alan, ultimately leads us to a self-awareness that we are more than just a physical body. We are a spirit, a soul, which is connected to all living beings. Our positive impact upon life is larger than we often imagine. We can contribute to the spirit of life even when the physical body fails.

The journey with Alan continues. Although it is more difficult to keep Alan hopeful and optimistic, we still manage to get there every now and then. The more I appreciate Alan, the more I am grateful for that moment. I find joy in just being with and serving him. His physical needs grow daily and the feeling of being trapped in those circumstances lurks in the background. However, when I manage to see his demands as a chance to serve, I get that calm feeling inside. Expanding the idea of serving to include people at work and in other areas of my life gives me calmness as well.

A Parent's Thoughts

For many years, I felt angry about Alan's disease and how it kept him from living a "normal" life. However, once I started seeing Alan's life and mine as journeys and not marathons, I began to feel less anxious. I heightened my awareness of everything happening around me, even the small moments, so I would not miss a thing. For a short time every day, try eliminating all of the expectations and must-do actions and silently observe your children at play. Something fun and unexpected may occur.

Alan and Me Together, Forever

The flight had been smooth. I prefer early morning travel since there is typically less noise from the other passengers. I used this travel time to write about an amazing event that recently occurred to me in San Francisco.

I was invited to speak at the Oracle Open World convention during the second week of October 2011. I talked about the effort I'd led at work to transform significant elements of the company, using the crisis created by the 2008 financial collapse in the United States to change how my company performed business and tracked cash flow. I used the lessons Alan and I learned over the years to guide my actions, particularly "It is not what happens to us but how we respond which defines who we are and what we accept."

Alan had always encouraged me to expand beyond the company I worked for. He had always wanted me to become known in the larger business world so that my ideas could be heard, leading to greater opportunities. When the invitation came to speak in San Francisco, I immediately saw this as a chance to satisfy Alan's wishes.

In addition to the presentation, I planned to have a meeting with one of the journalists at the event to begin writing an article that we would get published in a national magazine. We had met in Detroit several months earlier and talked about coauthoring a story about transformational change occurring across the country.

The convention lasted four days. After the third day, I still had not seen my journalist friend. Having already given my presentation the day before, I decided to spend the last day touring the city. With my new walking shoes all laced up, my mission was clear: walk before shopping. It was eight o'clock in the morning and the stores would not open until ten o'clock. I just needed to decide where I would walk, keeping in mind the location of the major shopping districts so I could buy the items my family had instructed me to get while in San Francisco.

I had several choices: head toward the new baseball park, mingle with the early morning people in the business district, or pursue the longest path toward Fisherman's Wharf. I still had not decided as I entered the street from my hotel. People were everywhere. I started walking down a street with fewer people, trying to avoid the crush of humanity. I walked several blocks until I saw a sign that said Fisherman's Wharf with an arrow pointing straight down the street I walked. My decision was made for me by the circumstances on the street.

My first landmark site was Hyde Park. Having just climbed several steep hills, I felt exhausted. I stopped for a coffee in a little shop, across from the park. Bright red umbrellas with black wrought-iron chairs contained within a fence of green shrubs lured me in. The owner had just washed the sidewalk so the air was fresh and moist. I sipped my drink, feeling sad about the lost opportunity to write the article. Alan had always pushed me to expand my expectations. I had failed to achieve that this time.

I asked the waiter, a young man with long black hair and a dragon tattoo on his right arm, if he lived in the city.

He did. In fact, he presently was acting in a play down the street, hoping to build toward his desired career as an actor in Hollywood. I told him I was walking toward the wharf. He laughed.

"Why are you walking there? Take the trolley. In addition to two more steep hills, there will be a neighborhood that will not be very welcoming to a businessman this early."

Well, that comment took me by surprise. I still see myself as young, like a college kid, who does not attract attention. Life and all of its challenges have certainly changed me, but I never expected to be called out like that. I now look like the "establishment" guy I used to criticize. Life can be cruel.

I stepped on to the next trolley and paid my fare. The older guy who took my money just stared at me.

"Did I give you enough money? I thought it was two dollars."

"People like you typically give me a tip. You look like you have the money."

I did not give him a tip. I was now angry. I was just trying to be anonymous, taking an early morning walk. This journey was turning out to be very different than expected. The trolley took me to the entrance of the wharf. Except for an elderly couple, I was the only one walking down the street of closed shops. After taking a few pictures of Alcatraz and buying a souvenir for Lili at a small T-shirt shop, I decided to start walking back to the trolley station.

I thought to myself, *so much for just following the flow to see what life will give you.* Before I walked more than one block back, I saw an open shop. "San Francisco's Famous Sour Dough Bread" read the sign above the door. *Okay,* I thought, *might as well treat myself to a quick sandwich before I return to the convention area.*

There were two lines in the store. One line was for breakfast meals and the other was for drinks. I stood in line for the meals, keeping my head down to avoid any more strange encounters. I paid for my meal and turned around to buy a drink, nearly knocking over a person as I turned. She, apparently, had also been turning around and did not see me either. I looked up to apologize. She looked at me and said, before I could get a word out, "Bob, what are you doing here this early in the morning?" This lady was my journalist friend.

For the next hour, we talked about the article, planned the specific ideas to write about, targeted publications for the article, and set timing for completing the work. She had been ill the previous three days and had not attended any of the convention events.

I remembered the words of Camille, my charismatic spiritual friend, who once told me there is no such thing as coincidence. The plan of God will reveal itself to us if we are open to the possibilities and become aware of the people and events which occur daily in our lives. This experience reinforced in me how we must, sometimes, be prepared to allow events to come to us. Patience can truly be a virtue, a means to become more aware of what is happening in our daily lives.

I suddenly felt sad as I wrote about this in my journal. Normally, I could not wait to tell Alan about this experience, wanting to hear his interpretation of what had happened. He would certainly have had tremendous insight into how these events fit into a larger pattern. But I no longer have Alan physically with me.

He passed away July 5, 2010.

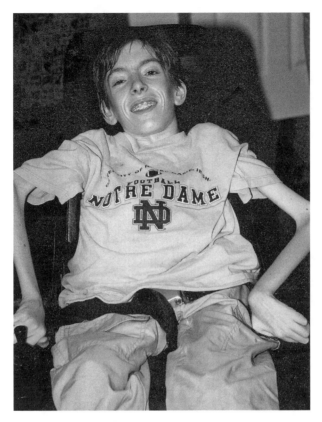

Alan watching football in family room, 2003.

The past year and a half has been filled with grieving and a very large sense of loss. Time does not heal. Instead, the loss rushes at and overwhelms my being whenever I have quiet moments. Alan took his last breaths right in front of Gwen and me. I panicked and yelled toward him as his breath became shallow. He briefly reopened his eyes and then closed them again. The nurse, who was there with us, told me that Alan loved me so much he actually came back for a brief moment when I yelled his name, not wanting to leave me.

The week before his passing away, Alan talked about many things, revealing thoughts and feelings never before discussed. He kept telling me how much the two of us were alike, almost the same person. He finally told me, after years of holding back, what his favorite summer trip had been and why. On the night before he left us, Alan told Gwen and me how much he always believed in possibilities. He felt there was nothing in life he could not accomplish, and he thanked Gwen and me for creating the right expectations in the family. He also repeated to me the need to expand, to not be just a local guy my whole life.

I woke up startled the first night after his death. I heard Alan saying these words: "No fear, no doubt, no regret." This final message continues to reverberate in my heart: no fear (the future), no doubt (the present), and no regret (the past).

I now carry my Alan's memory and words with me wherever I go. The loss overwhelms me at times. We fought side by side.

One day, I will be with him again. Until then, I keep him with me through my actions and decisions, always asking, what would Alan say, how would he respond, what strength would he show in response to the ever-changing circumstances of life. Like Alan said during his final few days, how much he and I were almost the same person, we continue to march on together, but now he is in a spiritual realm and I remain in the physical world. I am now flying to conventions, writing articles, and expanding my business career, but my soul still sits next to my Alan, side by side, whether in the hospital room, at home in his bedroom, or watching baseball games at Comerica Park.

I sit ready to help, learn, and understand.

Photo by Matthew Gaston

R obert Omilian is presently Director of Information
Systems for a global automotive supplier and is a
frequent guest speaker at national business seminars. He
was a publisher of the start-up magazine *Detroit Performer*
and has been a freelance writer for various publications.
He has an MBA from the University of Michigan and a
B.A. in philosophy and economics. He lives in a suburb
of Detroit, Michigan.

For more information about Robert, please visit

www.robertomilianbooks.com or

www.facebook.com/BooksByRobertOmilian